SIMPLE SONGS

SUPER EASY SONGBOOK

ISBN 978-1-5400-8422-4

HAL•LEONARD®

Visit Hal Leonard Online at
www.halleonard.com

Contact us:
Hal Leonard
7777 West Bluemound Road
Milwaukee, WI 53213
Email: info@halleonard.com

In Europe, contact:
Hal Leonard Europe Limited
42 Wigmore Street
Marylebone, London, W1U 2RN
Email: info@halleonardeurope.com

In Australia, contact:
Hal Leonard Australia Pty. Ltd.
4 Lentara Court
Cheltenham, Victoria, 3192 Australia
Email: info@halleonard.com.au

All My Loving

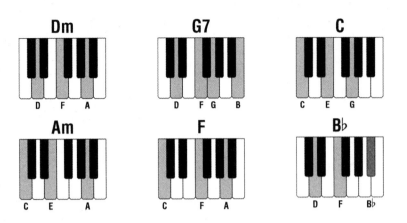

Words and Music by John Lennon
and Paul McCartney

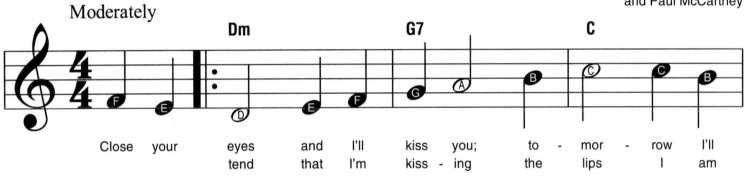

Close your eyes and I'll kiss you; to - mor - row I'll
tend that I'm kiss - ing the lips I am

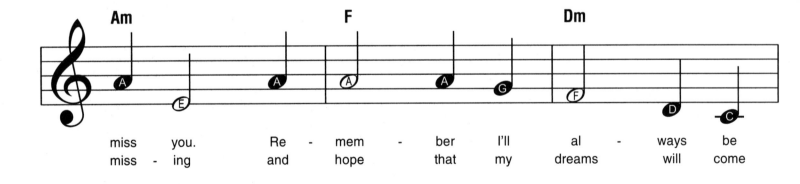

miss you. Re - mem - ber I'll al - ways be
miss - ing and hope that my al dreams will come

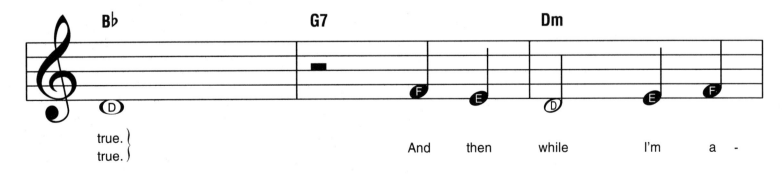

true. }
true. }

And then while I'm a -

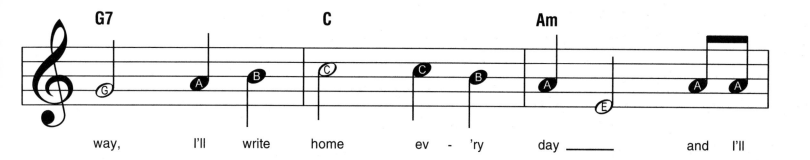

way, I'll write home ev - 'ry day _____ and I'll

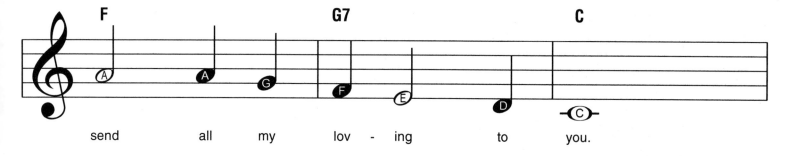

send all my lov - ing to you.

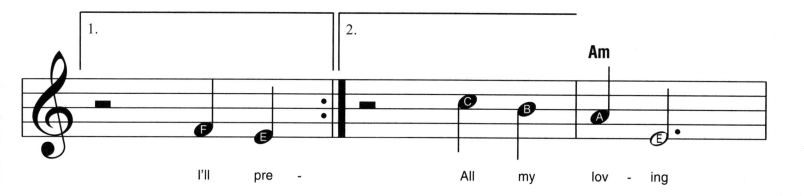

1. I'll pre -   2. All my lov - ing

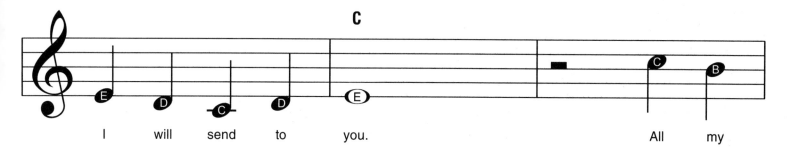

I will send to you.   All my

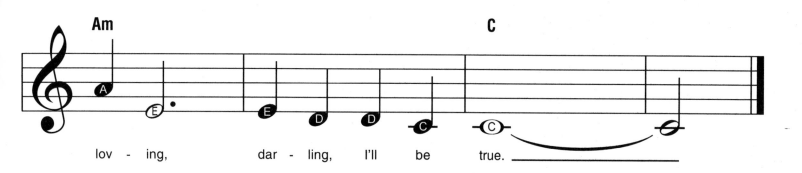

lov - ing,   dar - ling, I'll be   true. _____

Aloha Oe

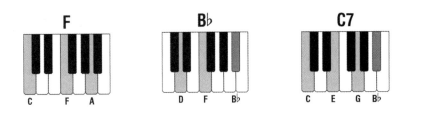

Words and Music by
Queen Liliuokalani

Moderately

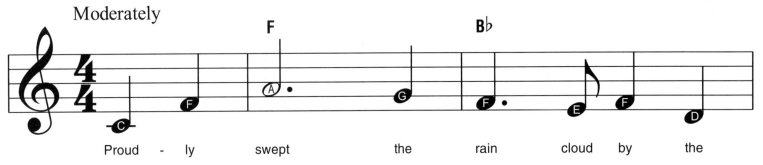

Proud - ly swept the rain cloud by the

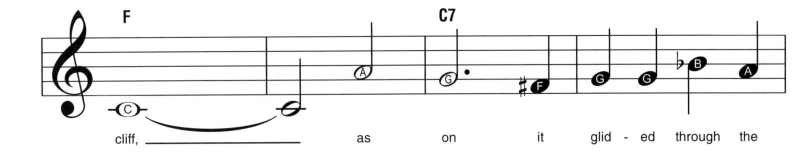

cliff, _____ as on it glid - ed through the

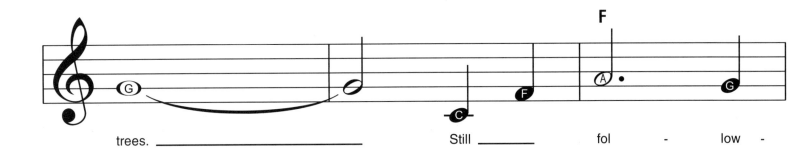

trees. _____ Still _____ fol - low -

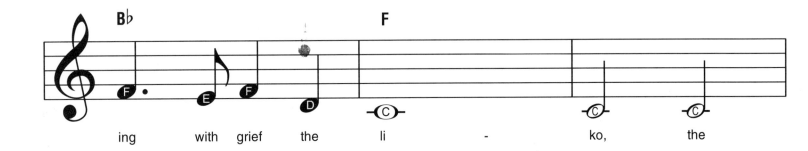

ing with grief the li - ko, the

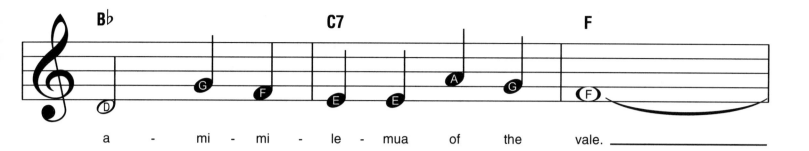

a - mi - mi - le - mua of the vale. _____

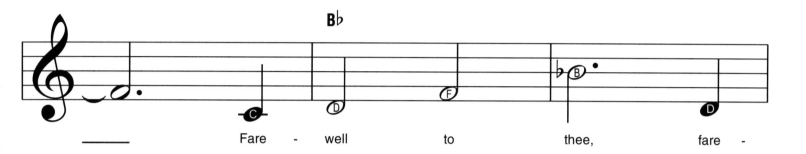

_____ Fare - well to thee, fare -

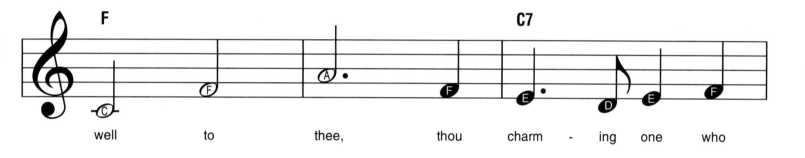

well to thee, thou charm - ing one who

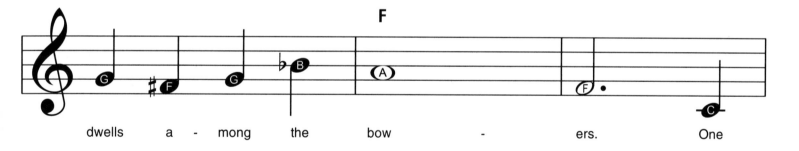

dwells a - mong the bow - ers. One

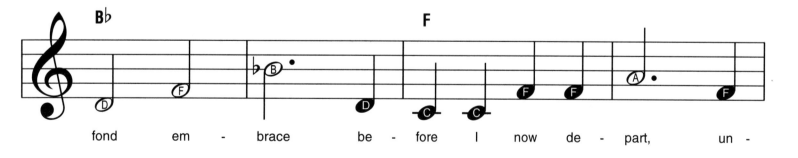

fond em - brace be - fore I now de - part, un -

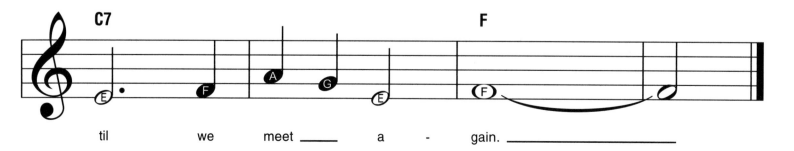

til we meet _____ a - gain. _____

Beauty and the Beast

from BEAUTY AND THE BEAST

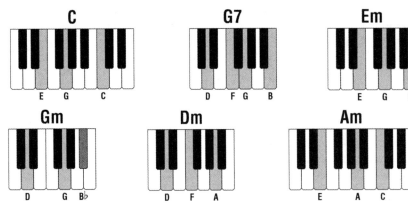

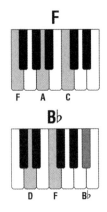

Music by Alan Menken
Lyrics by Howard Ashman

Moderately slow

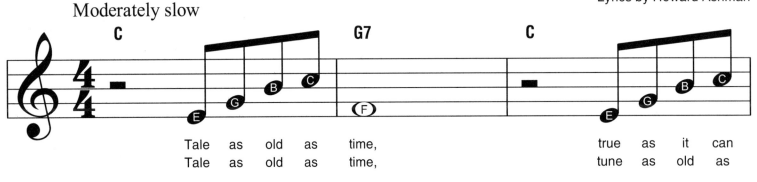

Tale as old as time,   true as it can
Tale as old as time,   tune as old as

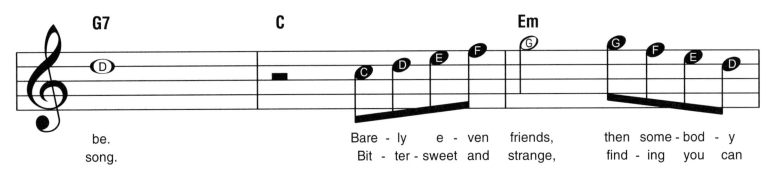

be.   Bare - ly e - ven friends,   then some - bod - y
song.   Bit - ter - sweet and strange,   find - ing you can

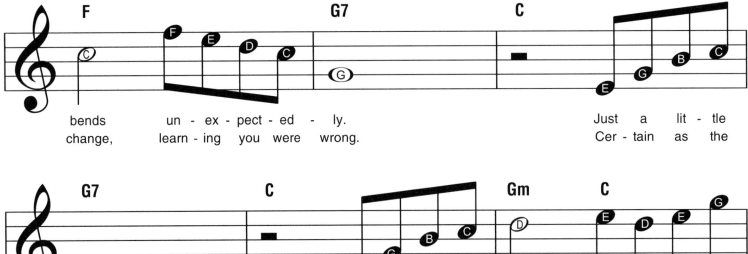

bends   un - ex - pect - ed - ly.   Just a lit - tle
change,   learn - ing you were wrong.   Cer - tain as the

change;   small, to say the least.   Both a lit - tle
sun   ris - ing in the east,   tale as old as

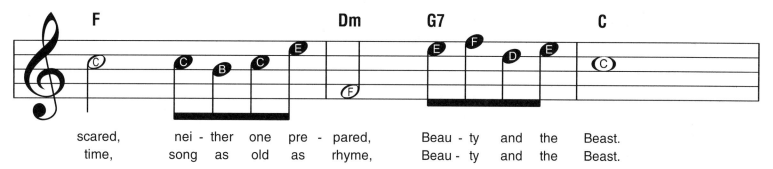

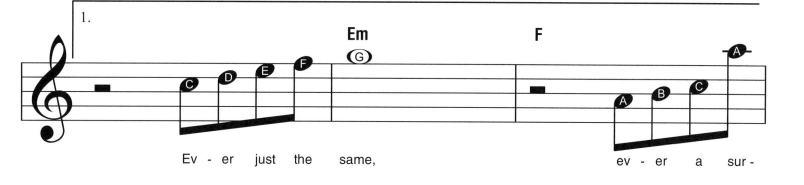

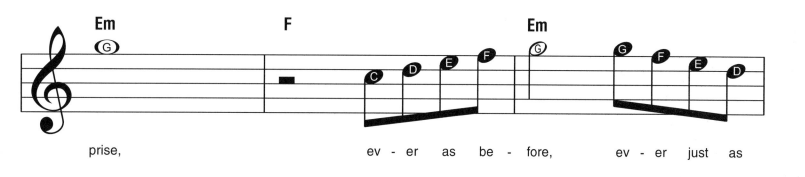

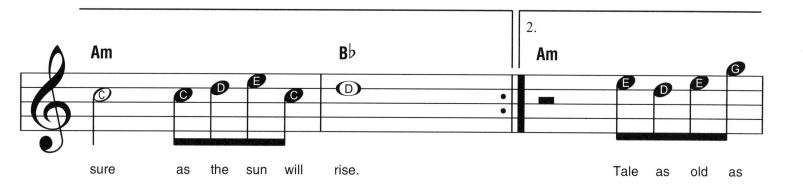

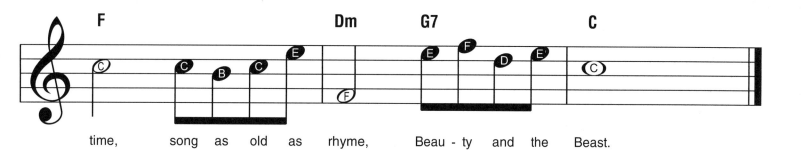

Blowin' in the Wind

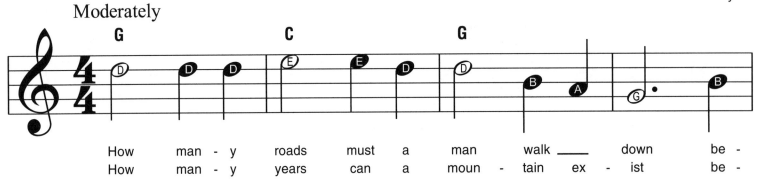

Words and Music by
Bob Dylan

Moderately

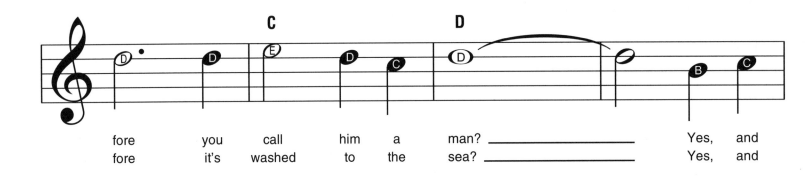

How man - y roads must a man walk ___ down be -
How man - y years can a moun - tain ex - ist be -

fore you call him a man? _____ Yes, and
fore it's washed to the sea? _____ Yes, and

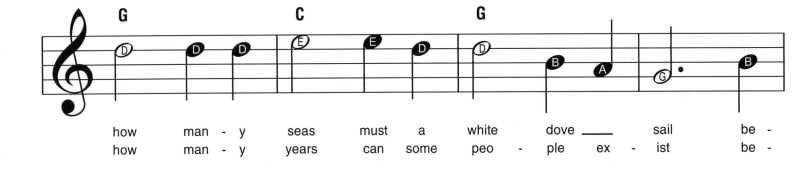

how man - y seas must a white dove ___ sail be -
how man - y years can some peo - ple ex - ist be -

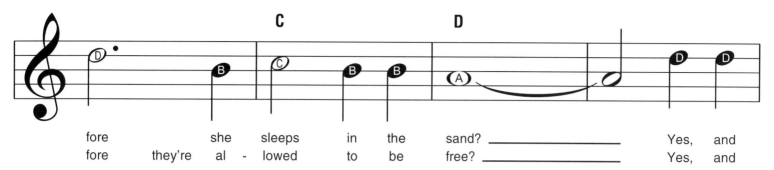

fore — she sleeps in the sand? _____ Yes, and
fore they're al - lowed to be free? _____ Yes, and

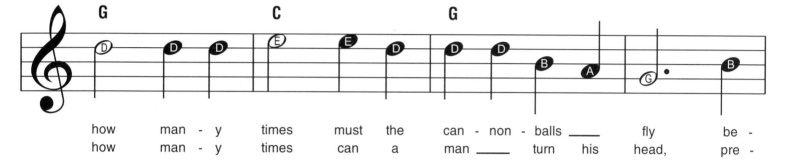

how man - y times must the can - non - balls ____ fly be -
how man - y times can a man ____ turn his head, pre -

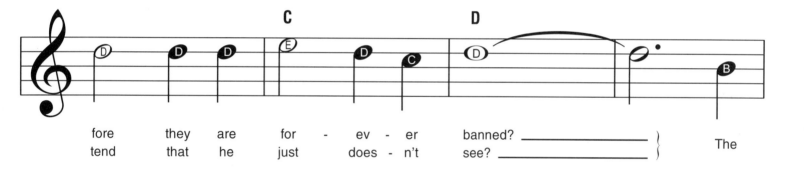

fore they are for - ev - er banned? _____ }
tend that he just does - n't see? _____ } The

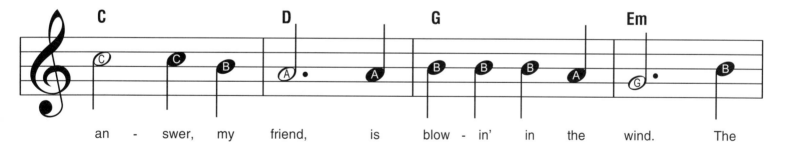

an - swer, my friend, is blow - in' in the wind. The

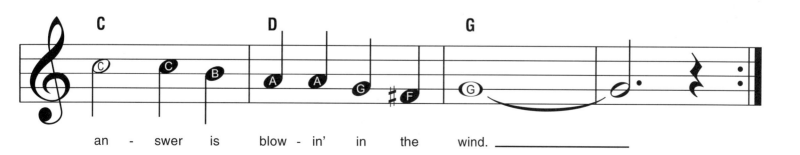

an - swer is blow - in' in the wind. _____

Blue Eyes Crying in the Rain

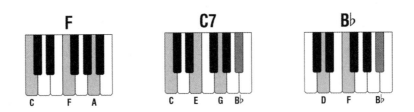

Words and Music by
Fred Rose

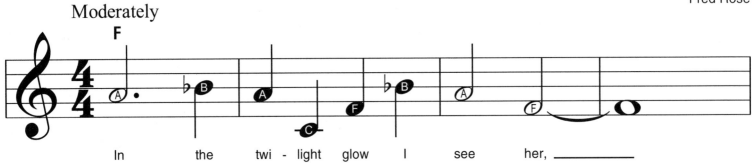

In the twi - light glow I see her, _____

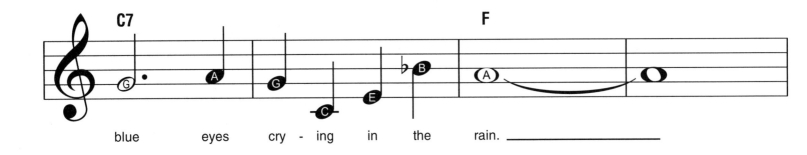

blue eyes cry - ing in the rain. _____

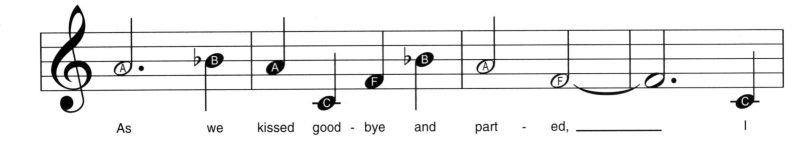

As we kissed good - bye and part - ed, _____ I

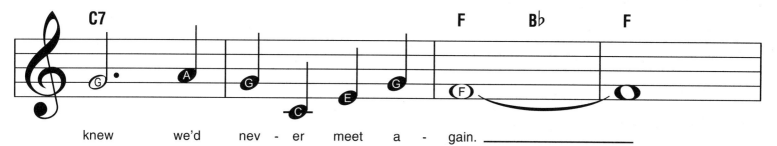

knew we'd nev - er meet a - gain. _____

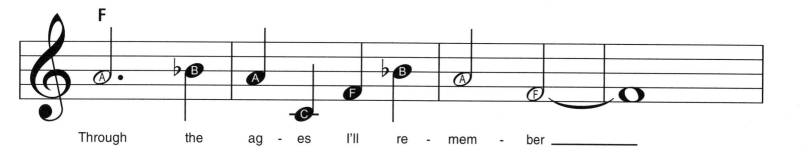

Love is like a dy - ing em - ber; _____

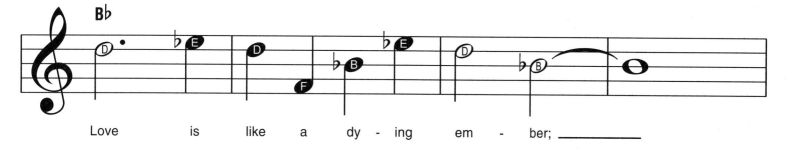

on - ly mem - o - ries re - main. _____

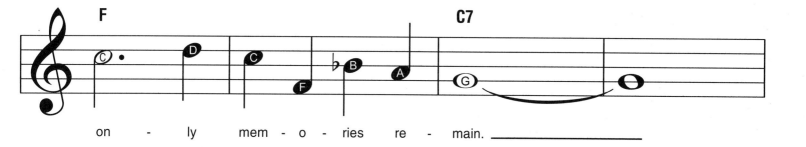

Through the ag - es I'll re - mem - ber _____

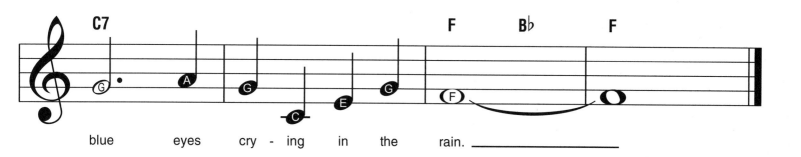

blue eyes cry - ing in the rain. _____

Bridge Over Troubled Water

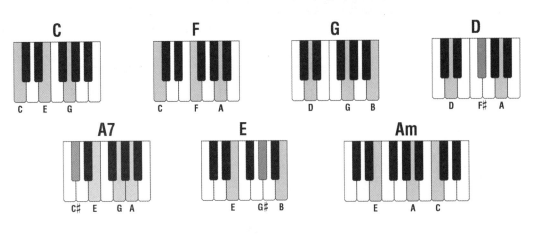

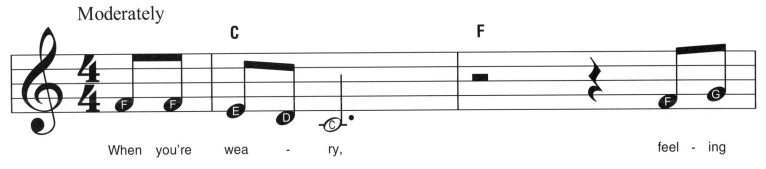

Words and Music by
Paul Simon

Moderately

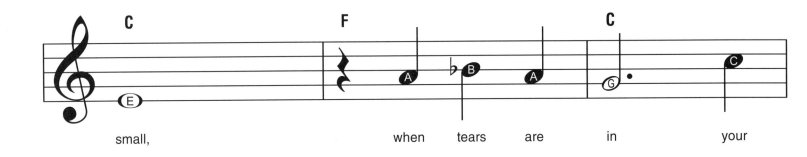

When you're wea - ry, feel - ing small, when tears are in your

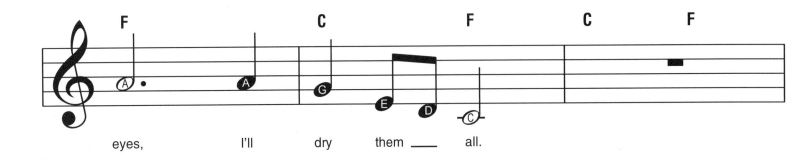

eyes, I'll dry them ___ all.

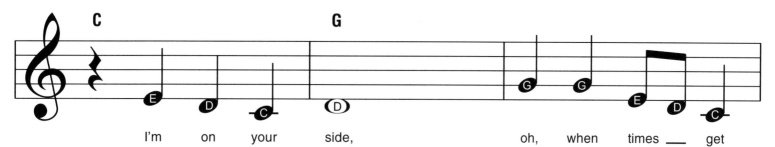

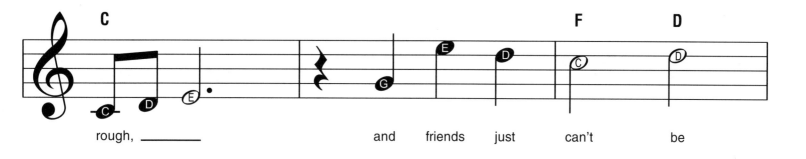

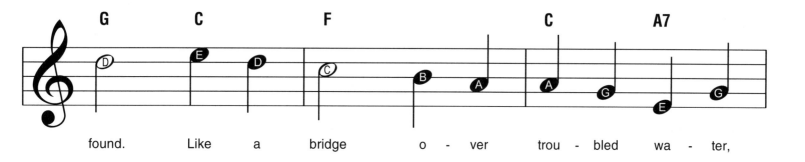

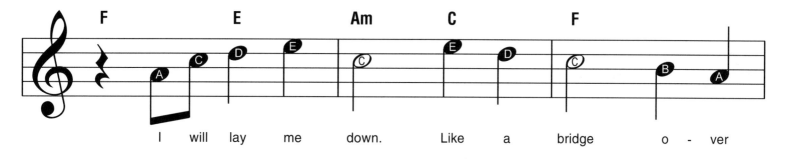

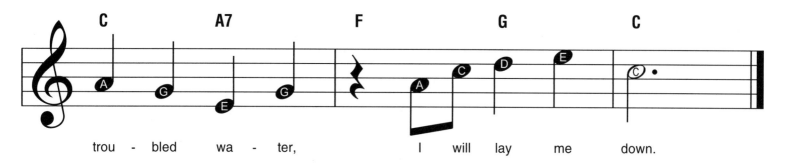

Bye Bye Love

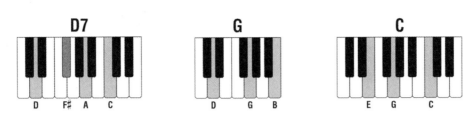

Words and Music by Felice Bryant
and Boudleaux Bryant

There goes my ba - by _____ with some - one new.

She looks so hap - py, _____ I sure am

blue. She was my ba - by _____

_____ till he stepped in. Good - bye to

ro - mance _____ that might have been. _____

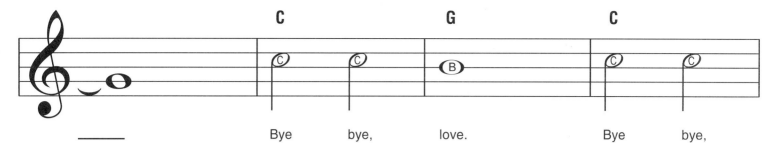

Bye bye, love. Bye bye,

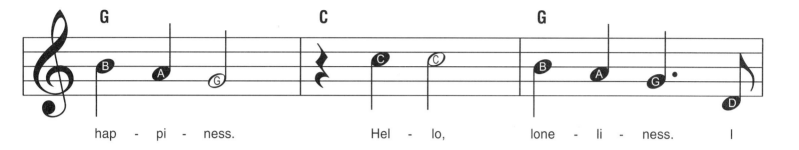

hap - pi - ness. Hel - lo, lone - li - ness. I

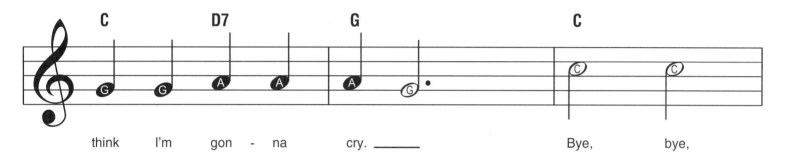

think I'm gon - na cry. _____ Bye, bye,

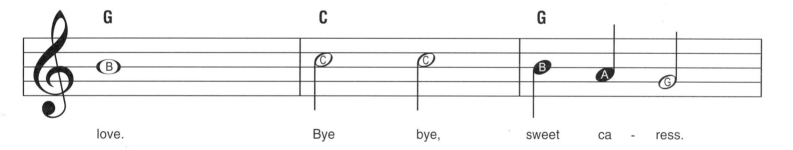

love. Bye bye, sweet ca - ress.

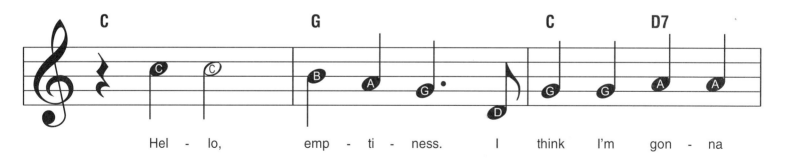

Hel - lo, emp - ti - ness. I think I'm gon - na

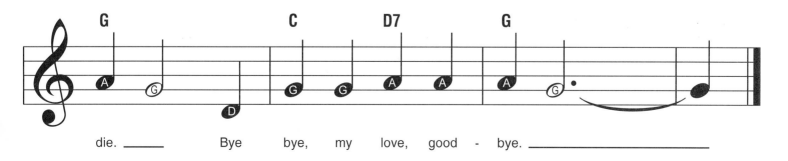

die. _____ Bye bye, my love, good - bye. _____

Catch a Falling Star

Words and Music by Paul Vance
and Lee Pockriss

Catch a fall - ing star and put it in your pock - et,

nev - er let it fade a - way. Catch a fall - ing star and

put it in your pock - et, save it for a rain - y day. For

love may come and tap you on the shoul - der some star - less

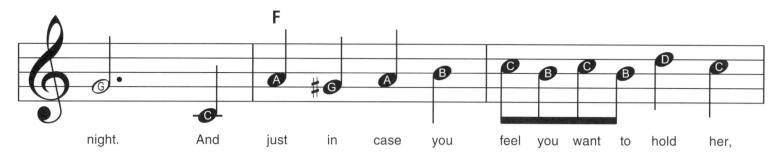

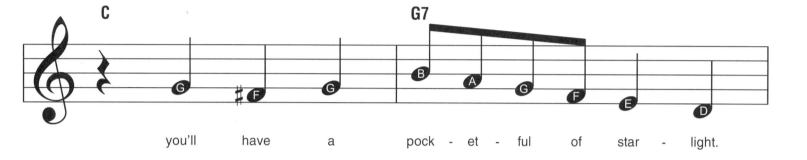

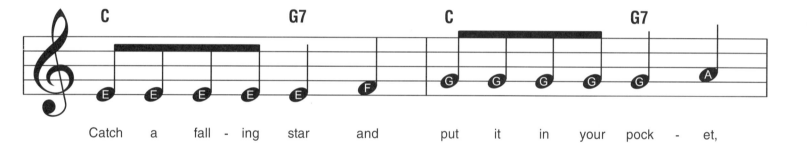

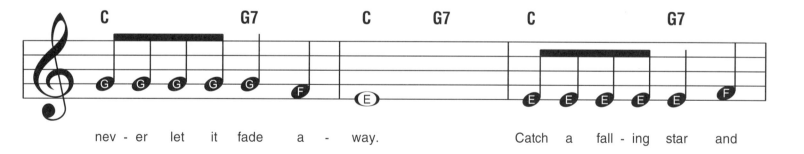

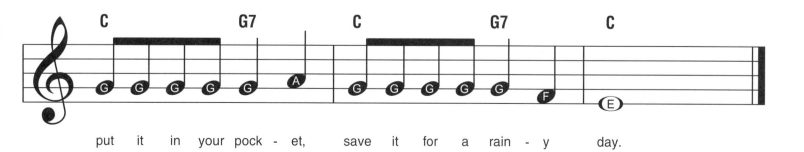

Deep in the Heart of Texas

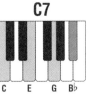

Words by June Hershey
Music by Don Swander

Happy Birthday to You

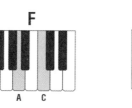
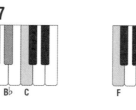

Words and Music by Mildred J. Hill
and Patty S. Hill

Do-Re-Mi
from THE SOUND OF MUSIC

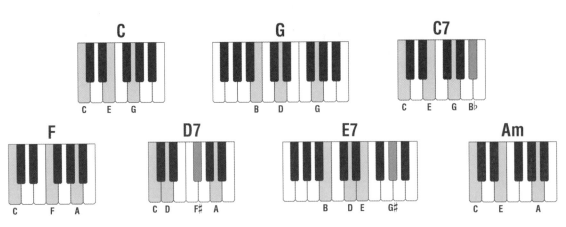

Lyrics by Oscar Hammerstein II
Music by Richard Rodgers

Brightly

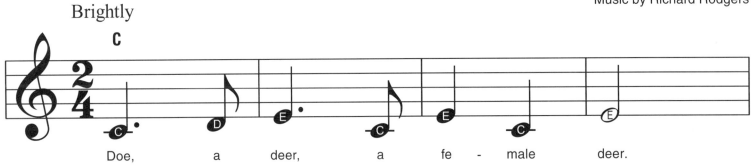

Doe, a deer, a fe - male deer.

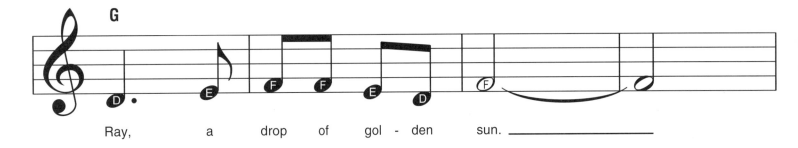

Ray, a drop of gol - den sun. _____

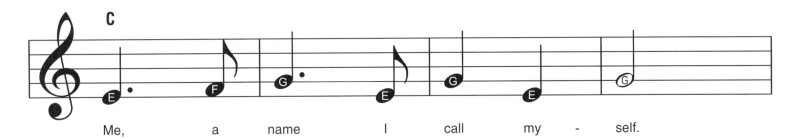

Me, a name I call my - self.

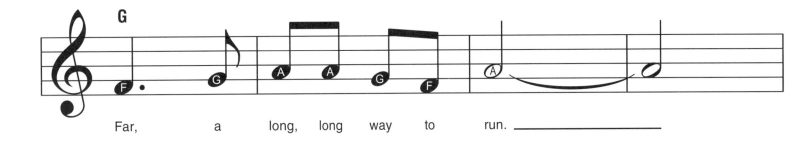

Far, a long, long way to run. _____

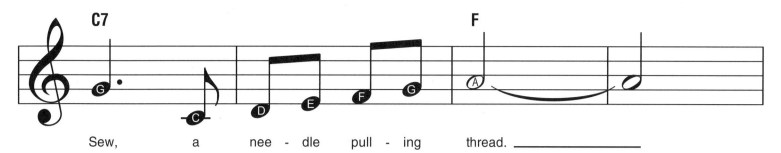

Sew, a nee - dle pull - ing thread. _____

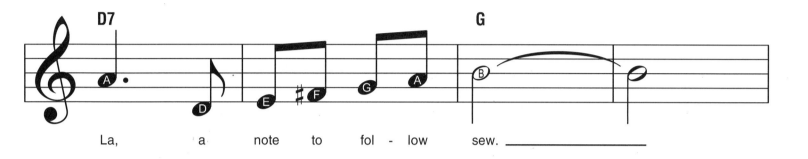

La, a note to fol - low sew. _____

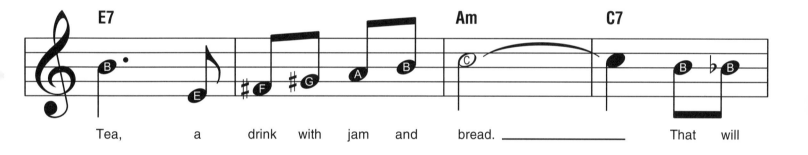

Tea, a drink with jam and bread. _____ That will

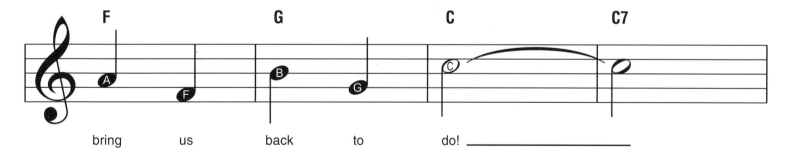

bring us back to do! _____

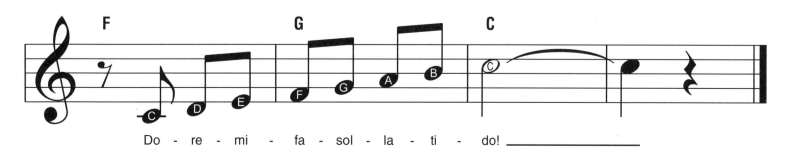

Do - re - mi - fa - sol - la - ti - do! _____

Down in the Valley

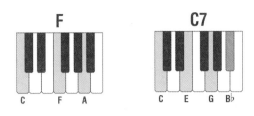

Traditional American Folksong

Moderately

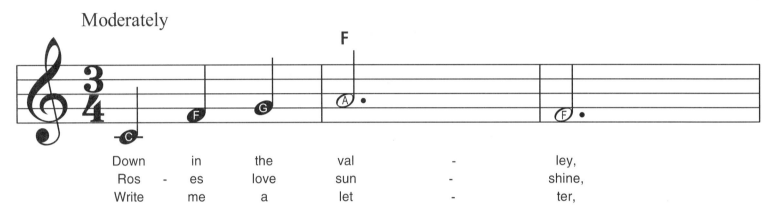

Down	in	the	val	-	ley,
Ros	- es	love	sun	-	shine,
Write	me	a	let	-	ter,

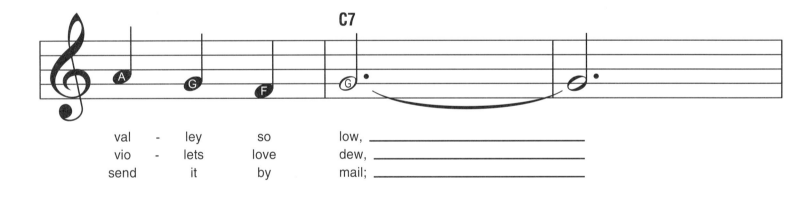

val	- ley	so	low, _____
vio	- lets	love	dew, _____
send	it	by	mail; _____

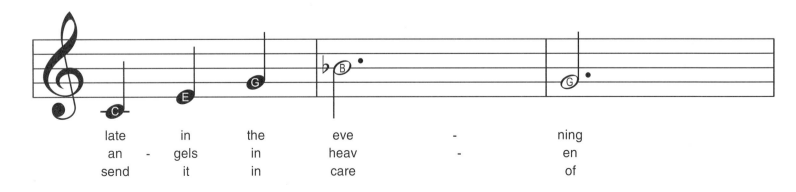

late	in	the	eve	-	ning
an	- gels	in	heav	-	en
send	it	in	care		of

F

hear the train blow. _____
know I love you. _____
Bir - ming - ham jail. _____

Hear that train blow - ing,
Know I love you, dear,
Bir - ming - ham jail - house,

C7

hear that train blow; _____
know I love you; _____
Bir - ming - ham jail, _____

hang your head o - ver,
an - gels in heav - en
send it in care of

F

hear that train blow. _____
know I love you. _____
Bir - ming - ham jail. _____

Eight Days a Week

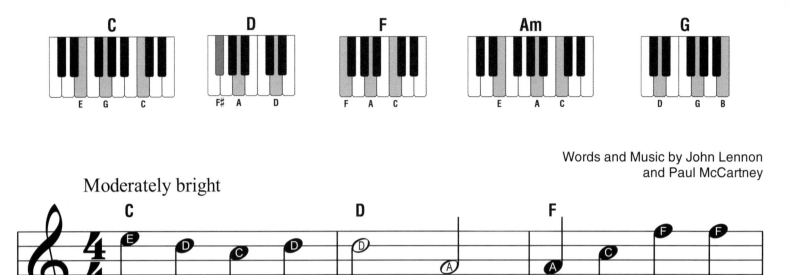

Words and Music by John Lennon
and Paul McCartney

Moderately bright

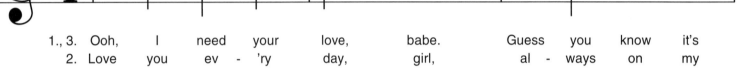

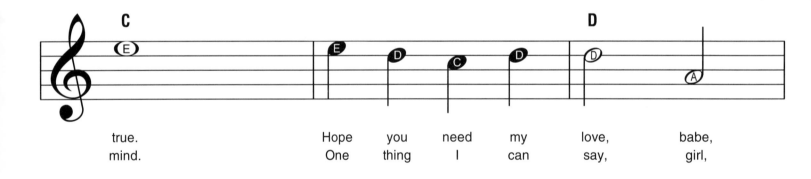

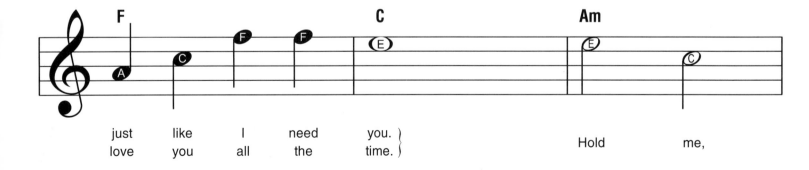

Fields of Gold

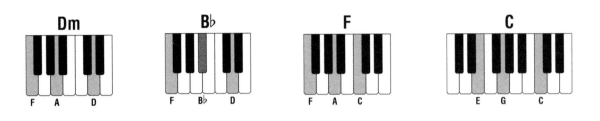

Music and Lyrics by
Sting

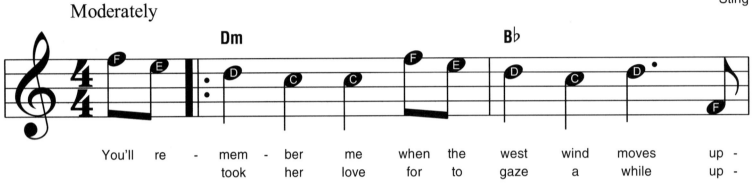

You'll re - mem - ber me when the west wind moves up -
took her love for to gaze a while up -

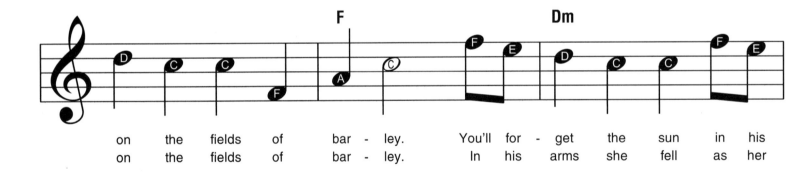

on the fields of bar - ley. You'll for - get the sun in his
on the fields of bar - ley. In his arms she fell as her

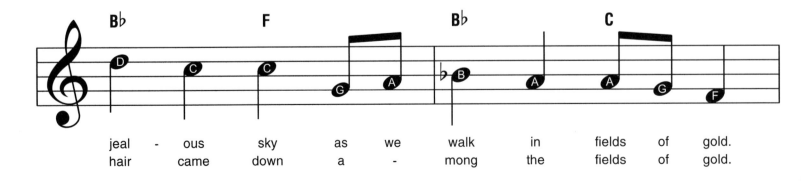

jeal - ous sky as we walk in fields of gold.
hair came down a - mong the fields of gold.

29

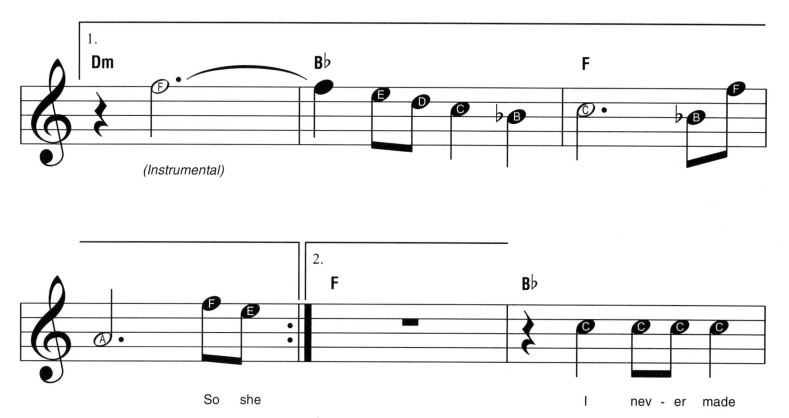

(Instrumental)

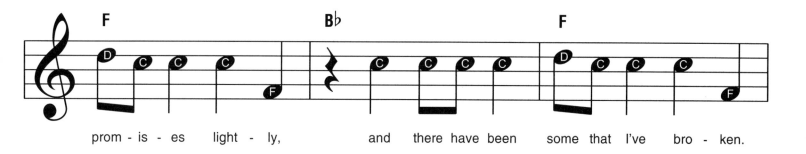

So she   I   nev - er made

prom - is - es light - ly,   and there have been some that I've bro - ken.

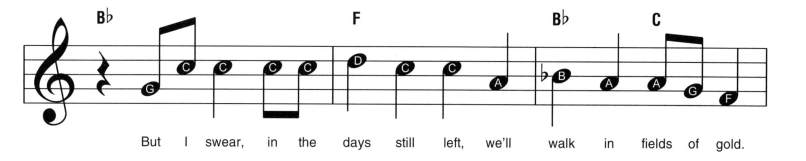

But I swear, in the days still left, we'll walk in fields of gold.

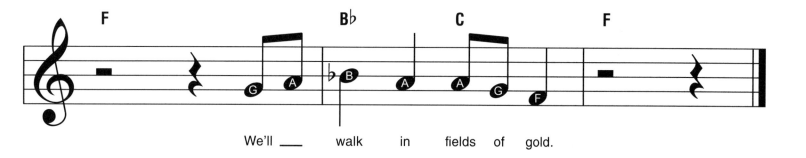

We'll ___ walk in fields of gold.

Good Riddance
(Time of Your Life)

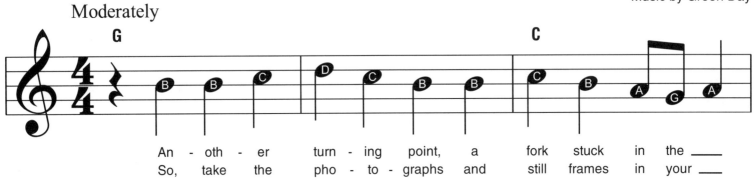

Words by Billie Joe
Music by Green Day

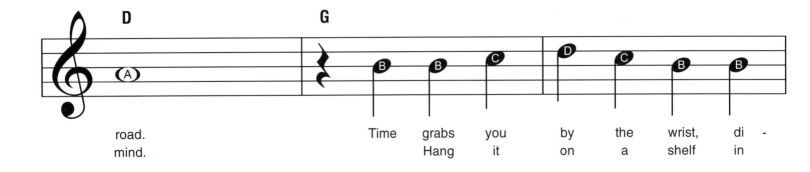

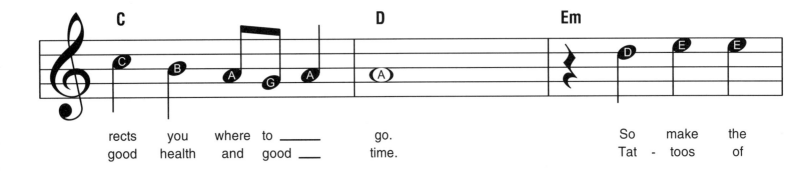

An - oth - er turn - ing point, a fork stuck in the _____ road.
So, take the pho - to - graphs and still frames in your _____ mind.

Time grabs you by the wrist, di - rects you where to _____ go.
Hang it on a shelf in good health and good _____ time.

So make the
Tat - toos of

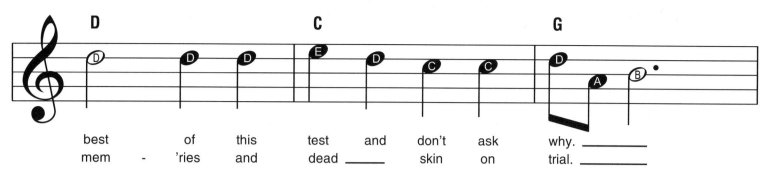

best of this test and don't ask why. _____
mem - 'ries and dead ____ skin on trial. _____

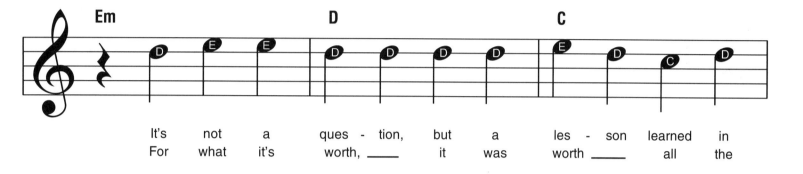

It's not a ques - tion, but a les - son learned in
For what it's worth, ____ it was worth ____ all the

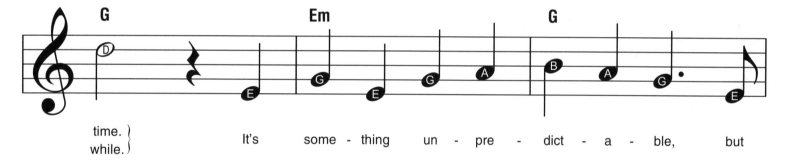

time.
while.

It's some - thing un - pre - dict - a - ble, but

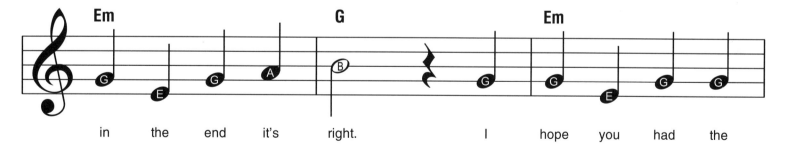

in the end it's right. I hope you had the

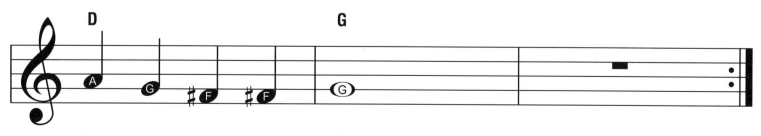

time _____ of your life.

Have You Ever Seen the Rain?

Words and Music by
John Fogerty

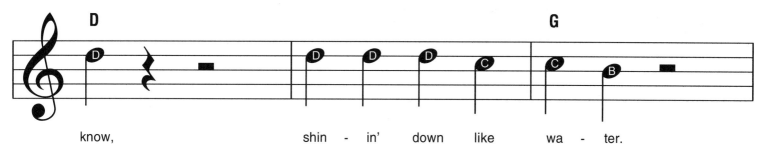

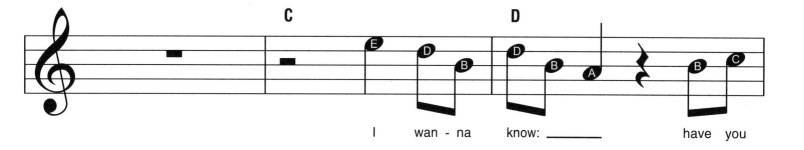

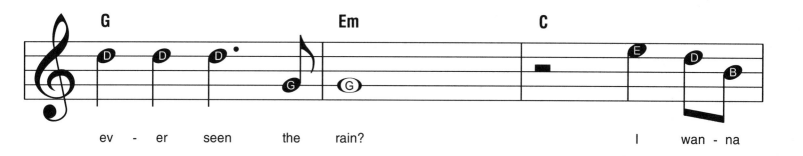

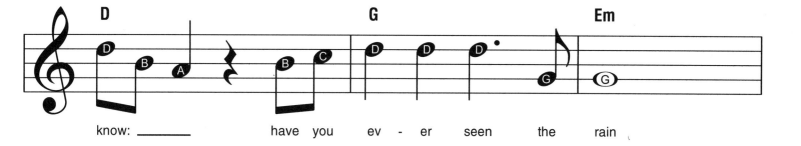

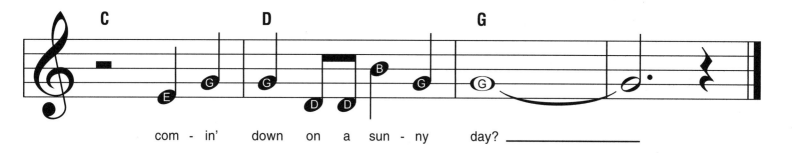

The Hokey Pokey

Words and Music by Charles P. Macak,
Tafft Baker and Larry LaPrise

How Much Is That Doggie in the Window

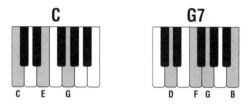

Words and Music by
Bob Merrill

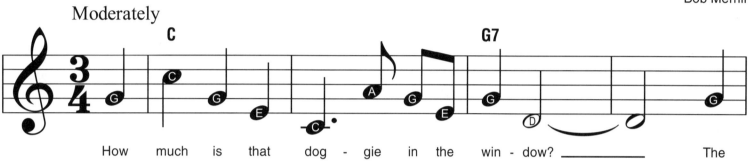

How much is that dog - gie in the win - dow? _____ The

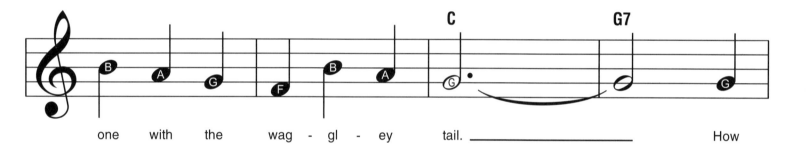

one with the wag - gl - ey tail. _____ How

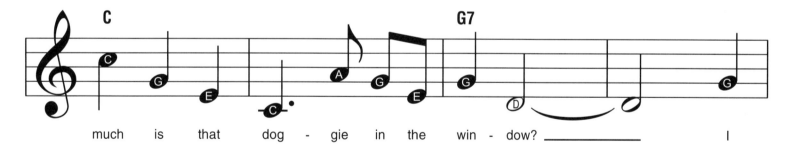

much is that dog - gie in the win - dow? _____ I

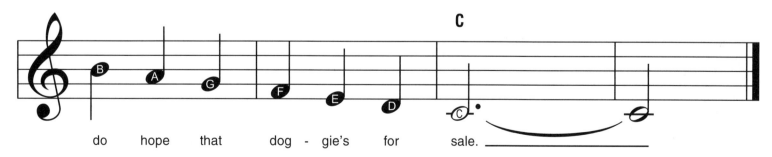

do hope that dog - gie's for sale. _____

Home on the Range

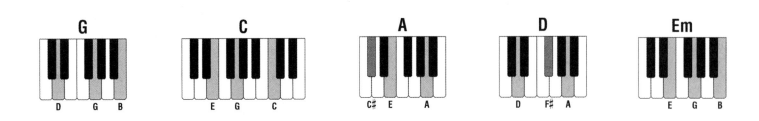

Lyrics by Dr. Brewster Higley
Music by Dan Kelly

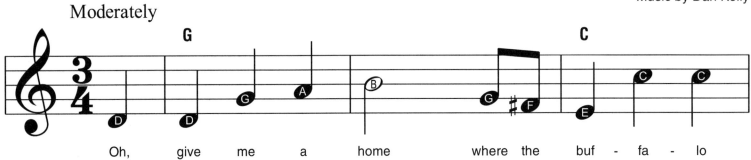

Oh, give me a home where the buf - fa - lo

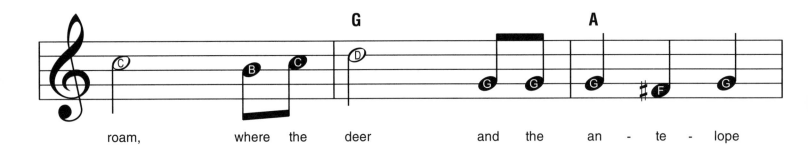

roam, where the deer and the an - te - lope

play. _____ Where sel - dom is

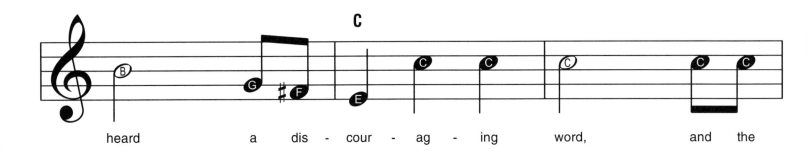

heard a dis - cour - ag - ing word, and the

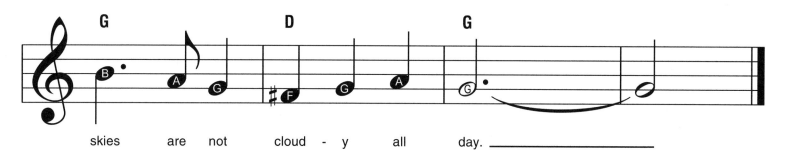

How to Save a Life

Words and Music by Joseph King
and Isaac Slade

Step one, you say, "We need to talk." He
walks, you say, "Sit down, it's just a talk." He smiles po -
lite - ly back at you. You stare po - lite - ly right on
through some sort of win - dow to your right as he goes

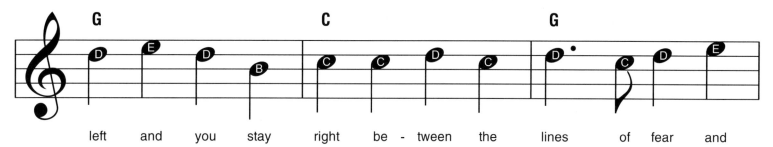

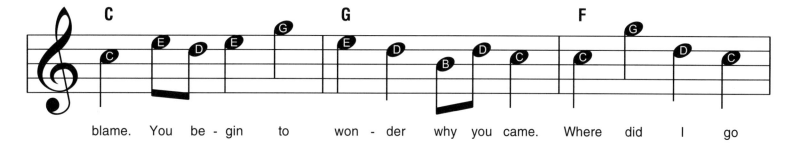

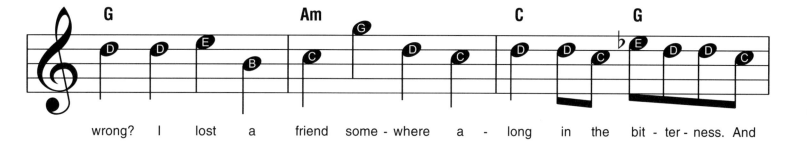

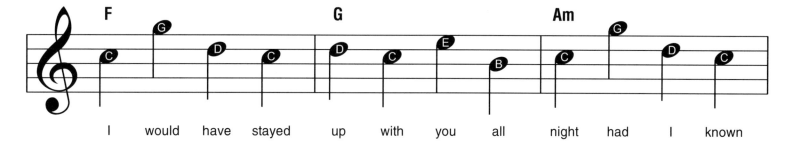

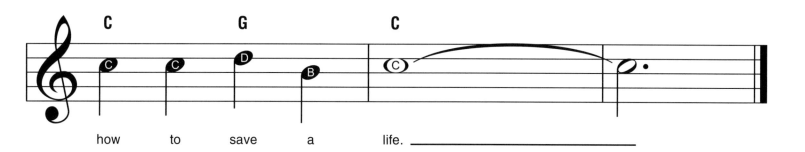

I Can See Clearly Now

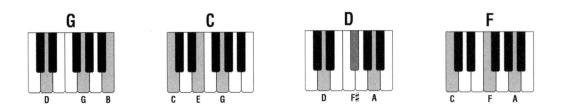

Words and Music by
Johnny Nash

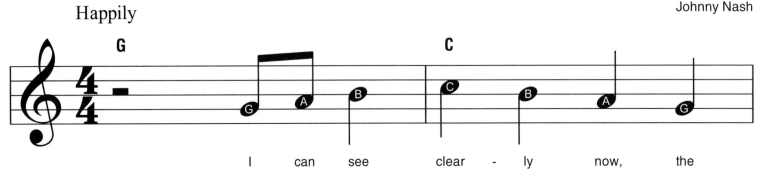

Happily

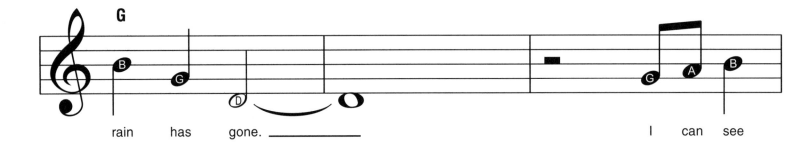

I can see clear - ly now, the
rain has gone. _____ I can see

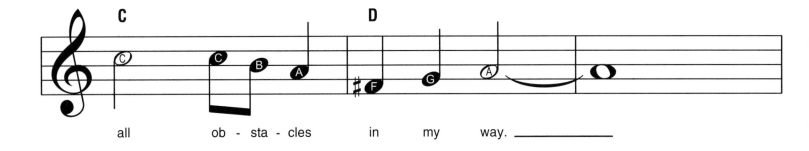

all ob - sta - cles in my way. _____

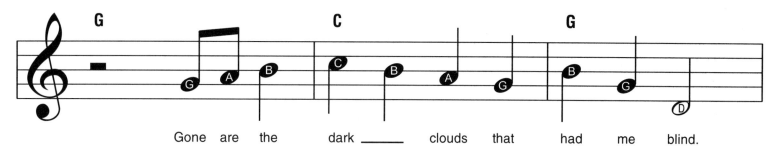

Gone are the dark _____ clouds that had me blind.

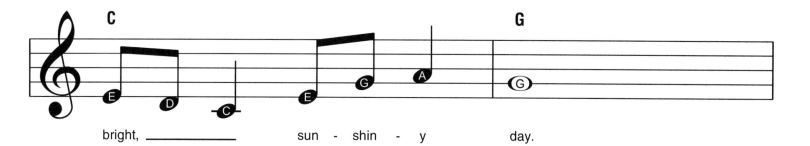

It's gon - na be a bright,

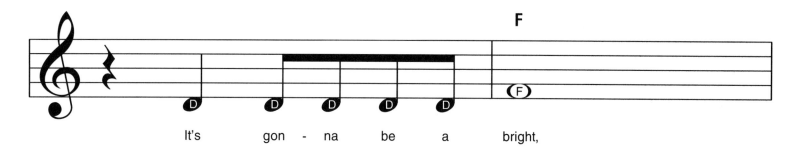

bright, _____ sun - shin - y day.

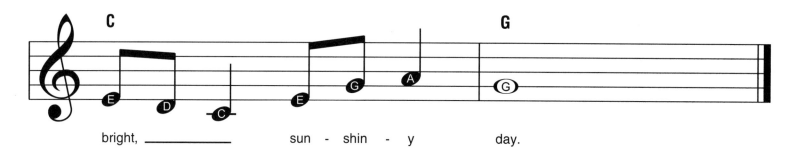

It's gon - na be a bright,

bright, _____ sun - shin - y day.

I Have a Dream
from MAMMA MIA!

Words and Music by Benny Andersson
and Björn Ulvaeus

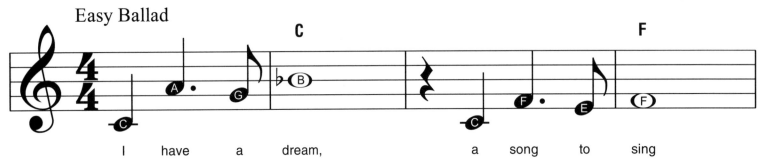

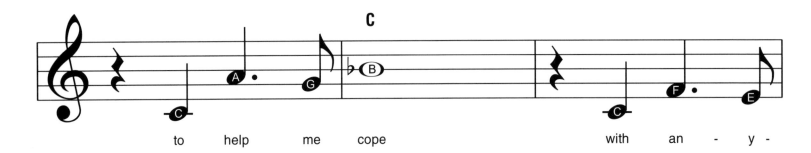

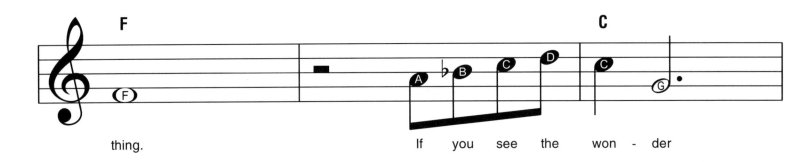

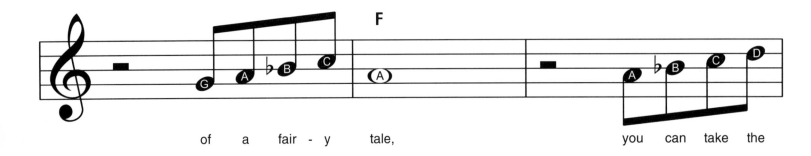

fu - ture   e - ven if you fail.

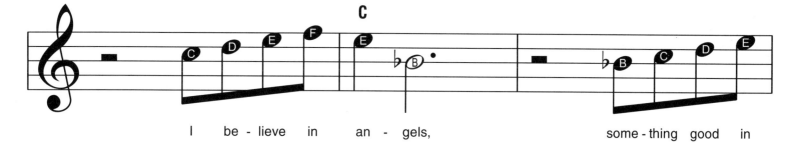

I be - lieve in an - gels,   some - thing good in

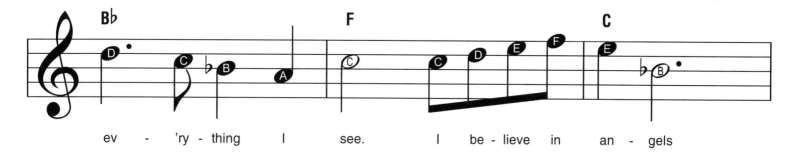

ev - 'ry - thing I see. I be - lieve in an - gels

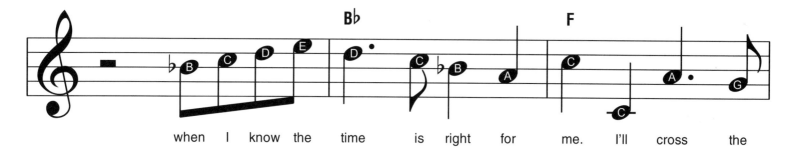

when I know the time is right for me. I'll cross the

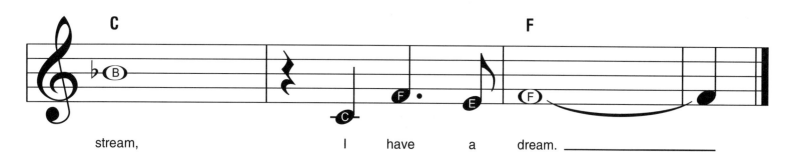

stream, I have a dream. _____

I Walk the Line

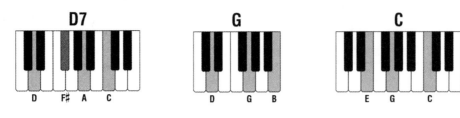

Words and Music by
John R. Cash

I'm So Lonesome I Could Cry

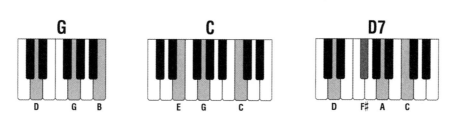

Words and Music by
Hank Williams

I'm Yours

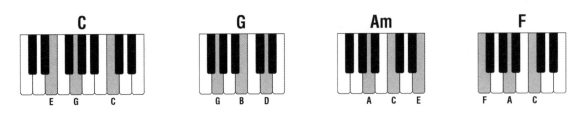

Words and Music by
Jason Mraz

Moderately fast Shuffle

Well, you done done me in; you bet I felt it. I

tried to be chill, but you're so hot that I melt - ed. I

fell right through the cracks. Now I'm try - ing to get back.

Be - fore the cool done run out, I'll be giv - ing it my best - est, and

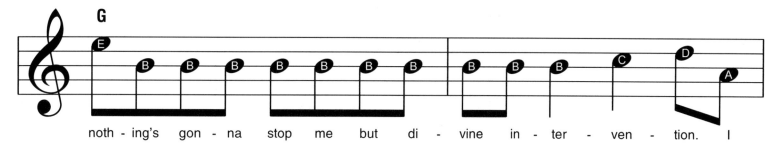

noth - ing's gon - na stop me but di - vine in - ter - ven - tion. I

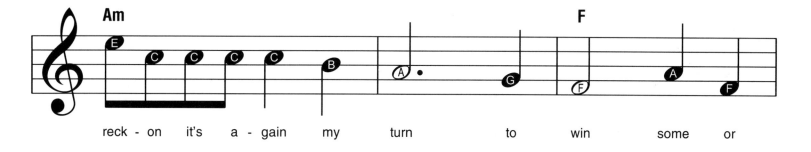

reck - on it's a - gain my turn to win some or

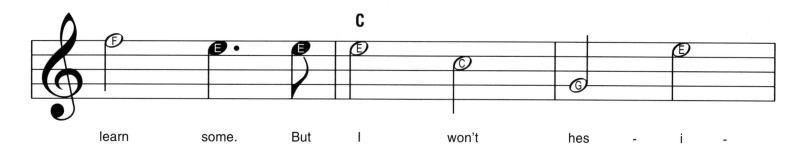

learn some. But I won't hes - i -

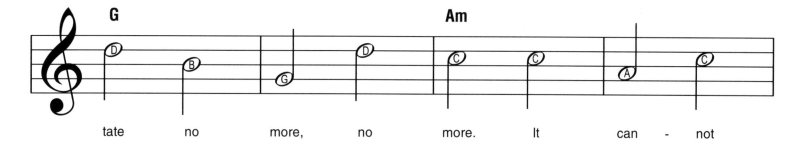

tate no more, no more. It can - not

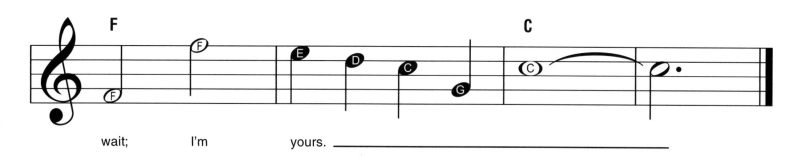

wait; I'm yours. _____

Jambalaya
(On the Bayou)

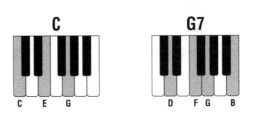

Words and Music by
Hank Williams

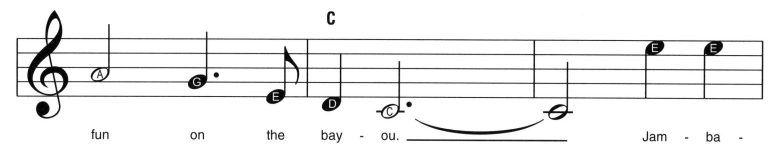

fun on the bay - ou. _____ Jam - ba -

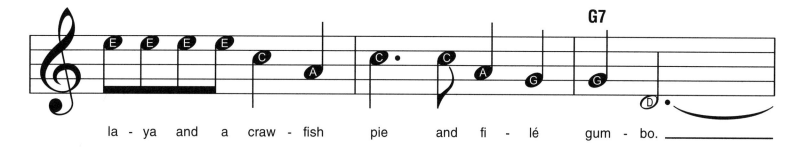

la - ya and a craw-fish pie and fi - lé gum - bo. _____

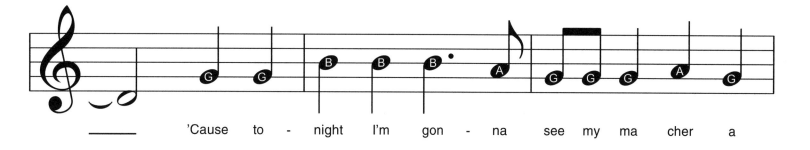

_____ 'Cause to - night I'm gon - na see my ma cher a

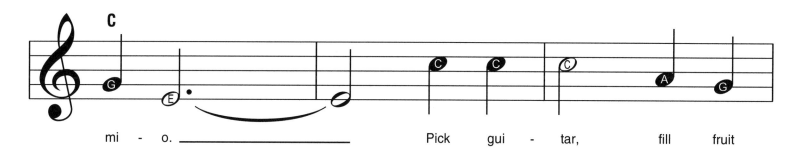

mi - o. _____ Pick gui - tar, fill fruit

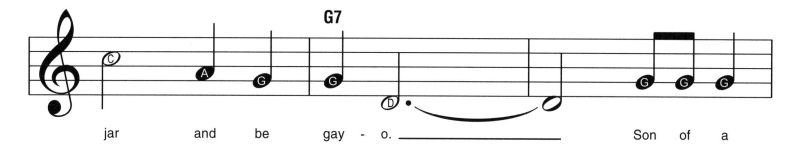

jar and be gay - o. _____ Son of a

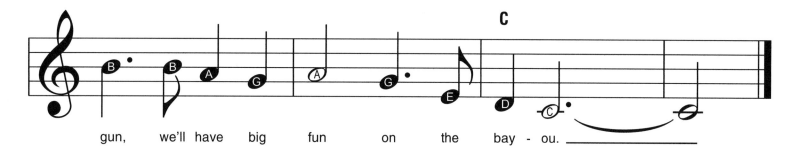

gun, we'll have big fun on the bay - ou. _____

The Lion Sleeps Tonight

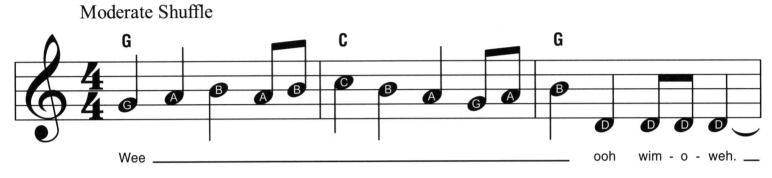

New Lyrics and Revised Music by George David Weiss,
Hugo Peretti and Luigi Creatore

Moderate Shuffle

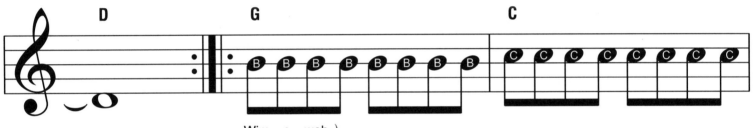

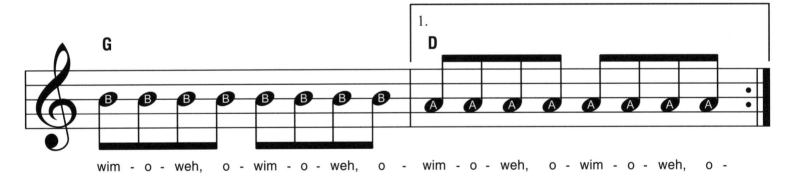

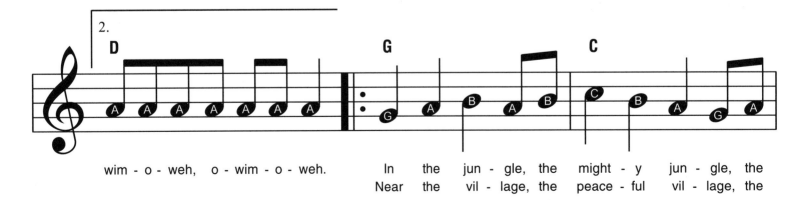

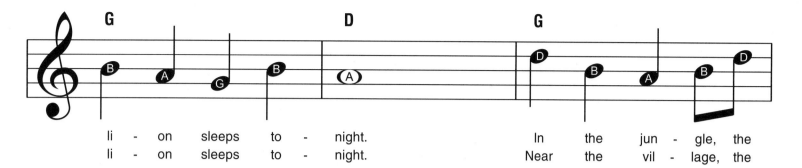

li - on sleeps to - night.
li - on sleeps to - night.
In the jun - gle, the
Near the vil - lage, the

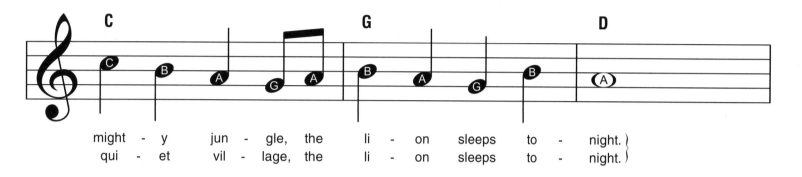

might - y jun - gle, the li - on sleeps to - night.
qui - et vil - lage, the li - on sleeps to - night.

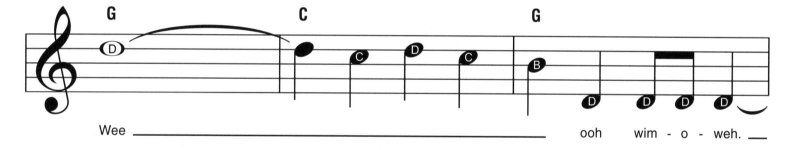

Wee _____ ooh wim - o - weh. ___

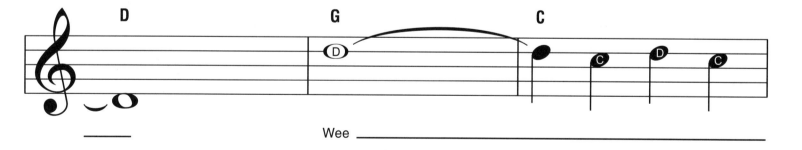

___ Wee _____

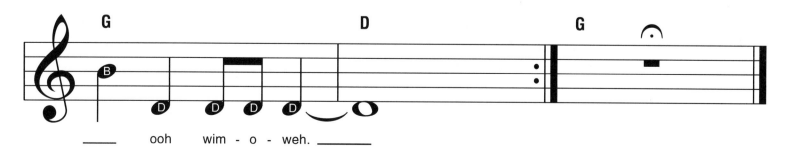

___ ooh wim - o - weh. _____

The Longest Time

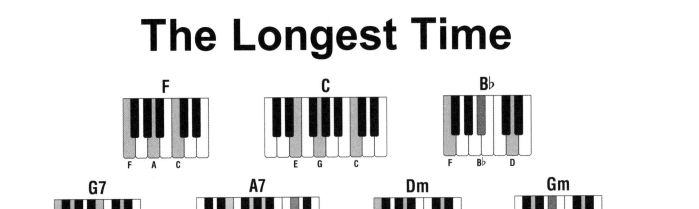

Words and Music by
Billy Joel

Moderate half-time feel

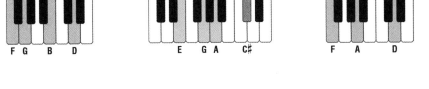

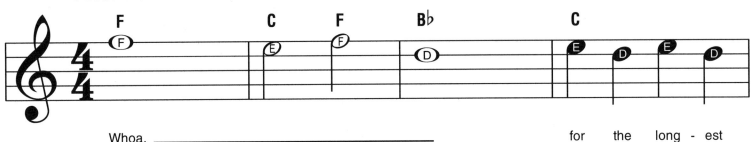

Whoa, _____ for the long - est

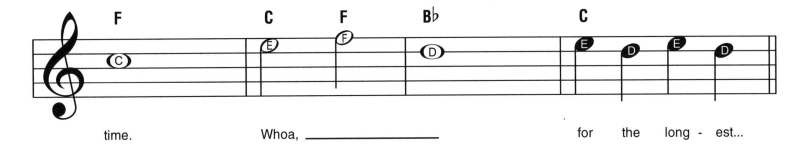

time. Whoa, _____ for the long - est...

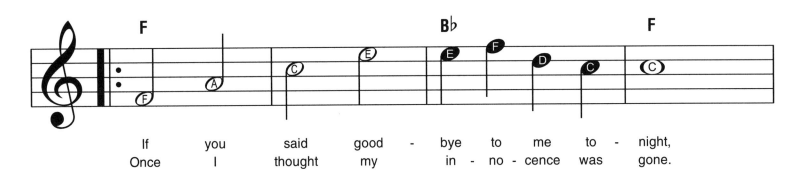

If you said good - bye to me to - night,
Once I thought my in - no - cence was gone.

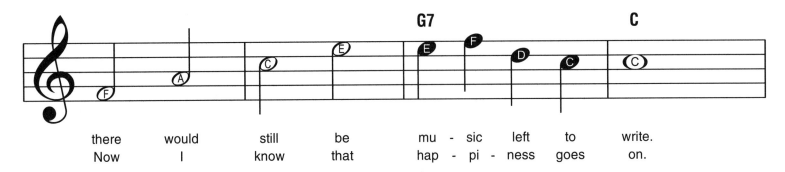

there would still be mu - sic left to write.
Now I know that hap - pi - ness goes on.

long - est time.
long - est time.   Whoa, _____

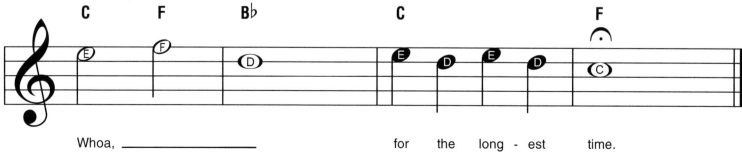

Whoa, _____   for the long - est time.

Love Me Tender

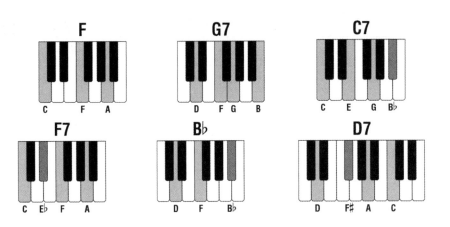

Words and Music by Elvis Presley
and Vera Matson

Moderately slow

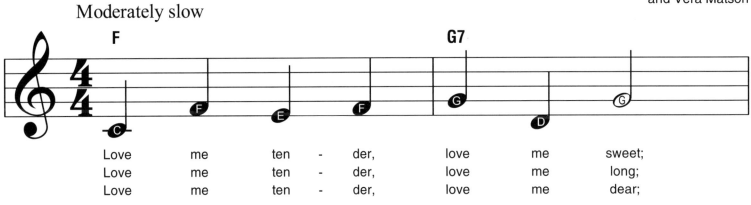

Love me ten - der, love me sweet;
Love me ten - der, love me long;
Love me ten - der, love me dear;

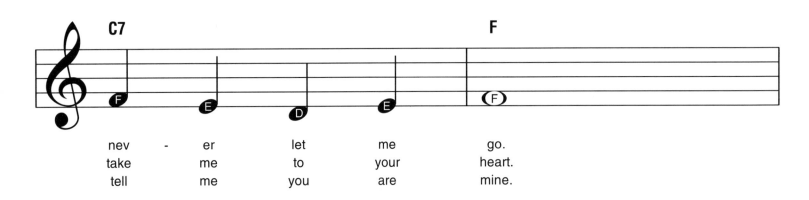

nev - er let me go.
take me to your heart.
tell me you are mine.

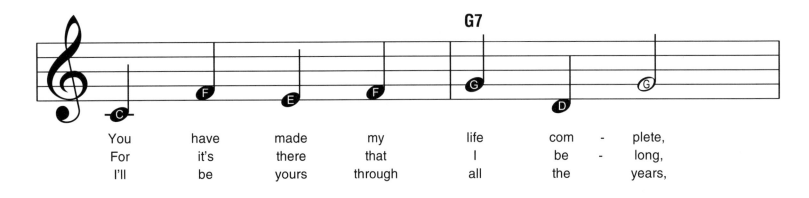

You have made my life com - plete,
For it's made there that I be - long,
I'll be yours through all the years,

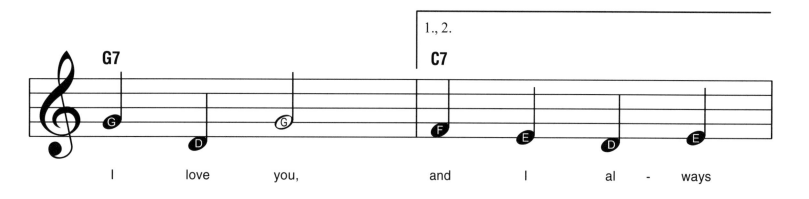

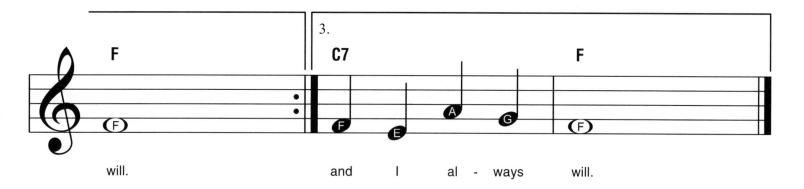

Mr. Tambourine Man

Words and Music by
Bob Dylan

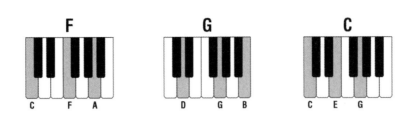

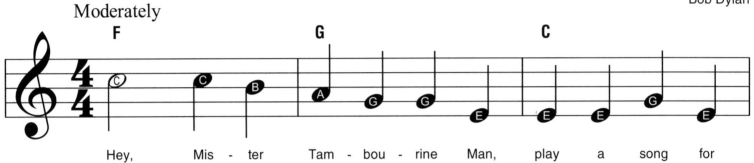

Hey, Mis - ter Tam - bou - rine Man, play a song for

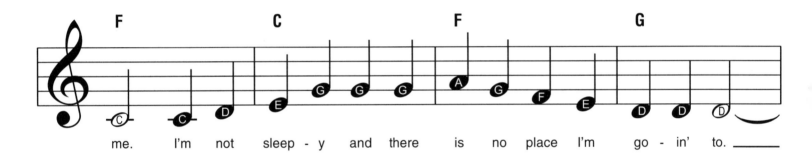

me. I'm not sleep - y and there is no place I'm go - in' to. ____

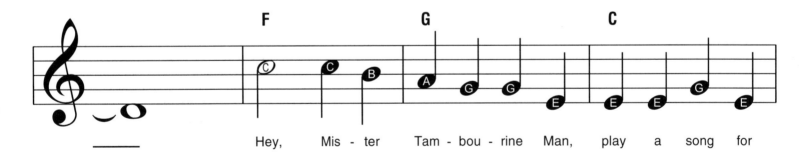

____ Hey, Mis - ter Tam - bou - rine Man, play a song for

To Coda

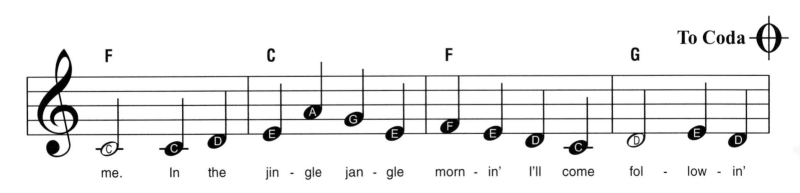

me. In the jin - gle jan - gle morn - in' I'll come fol - low - in'

Morning Has Broken

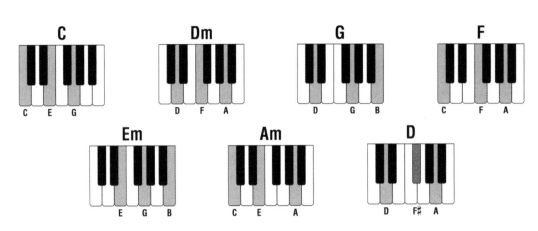

Words by Eleanor Farjeon
Music by Cat Stevens

Flowing
(no chord)

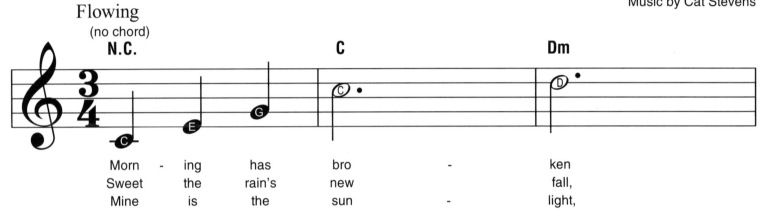

Morn - ing has bro - ken
Sweet the rain's new fall,
Mine is the sun - light,

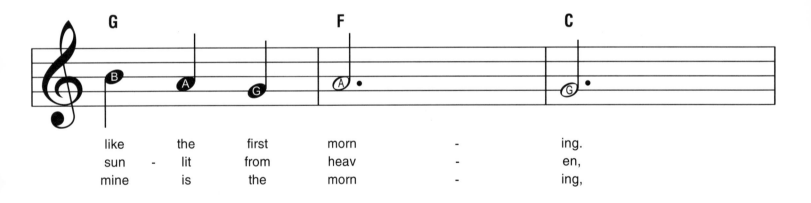

like the first morn - ing.
sun - lit from heav - en,
mine is the morn - ing,

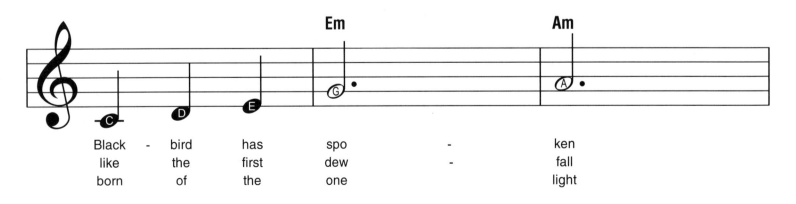

Black - bird has spo - ken
like the first dew - fall
born of the one light

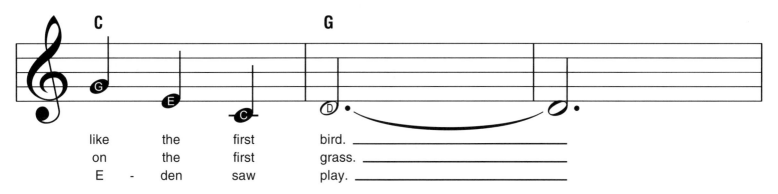

C · · · · G

like the first bird. _____
on the first grass. _____
E - den saw play. _____

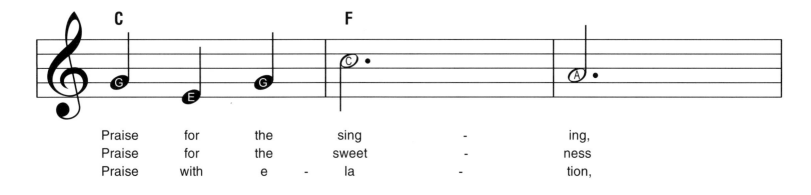

C · · · · F

Praise for the sing - ing,
Praise for the sweet - ness
Praise with e - la - tion,

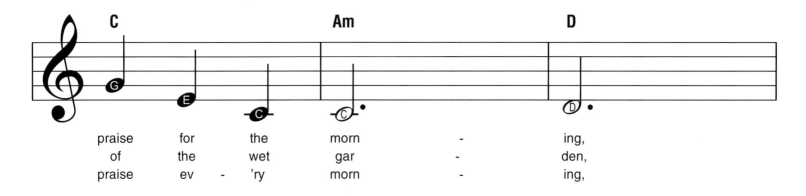

C · · · · Am · · · D

praise for the morn - ing,
of the wet gar - den,
praise ev - 'ry morn - ing,

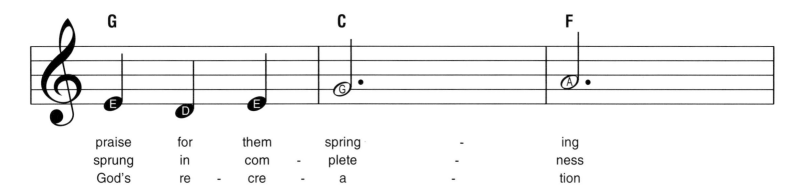

G · · · · C · · · F

praise for them spring - ing
sprung in com - plete - ness
God's re - cre - a - tion

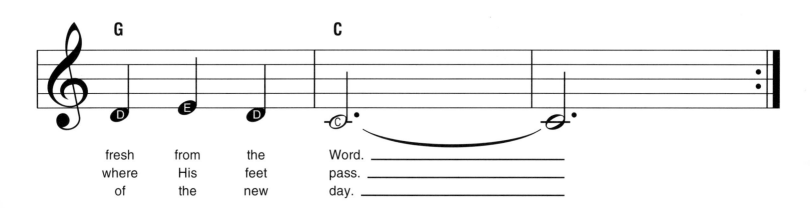

G · · · · C

fresh from the Word. _____
where His feet pass. _____
of the new day. _____

Norwegian Wood
(This Bird Has Flown)

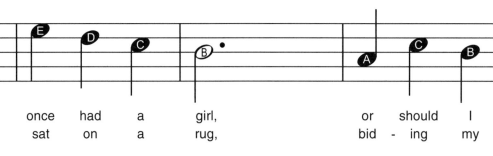

Words and Music by John Lennon
and Paul McCartney

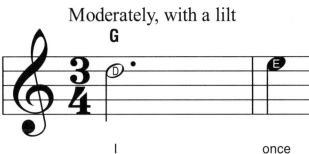

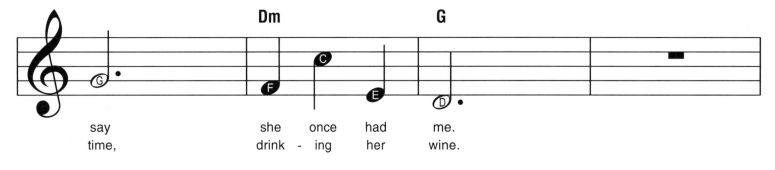

I once had a girl, or should I
I sat on a rug, bid - ing my

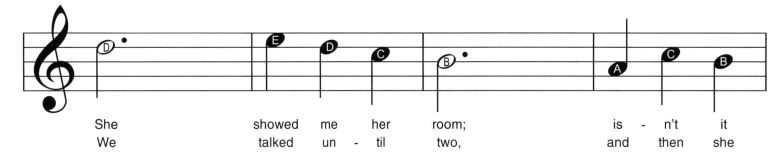

say she once had me.
time, drink - ing her wine.

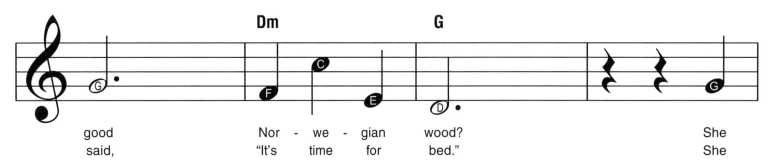

She showed me her room; is - n't it
We talked un - til two, and then she

good Nor - we - gian wood? She
said, "It's time for bed." She

Oh, What a Beautiful Mornin'

from OKLAHOMA!

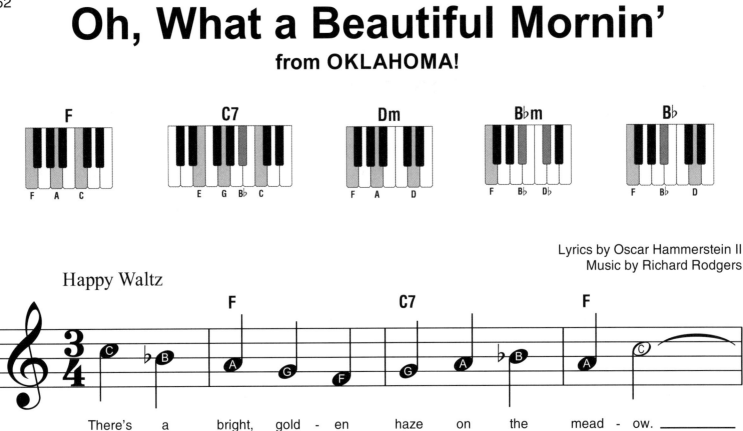

Lyrics by Oscar Hammerstein II
Music by Richard Rodgers

Happy Waltz

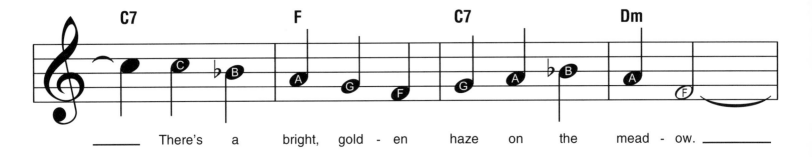

There's a bright, gold-en haze on the mead-ow. _____

_____ There's a bright, gold-en haze on the mead-ow. _____

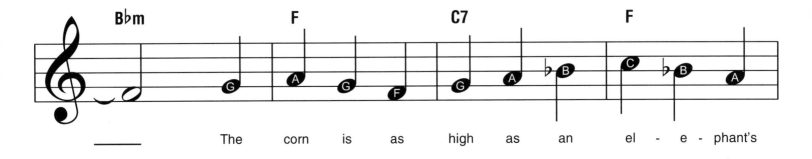

_____ The corn is as high as an el-e-phant's

63

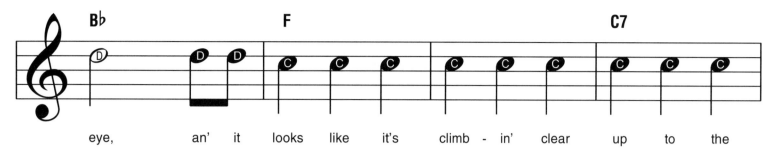

eye, an' it looks like it's climb - in' clear up to the

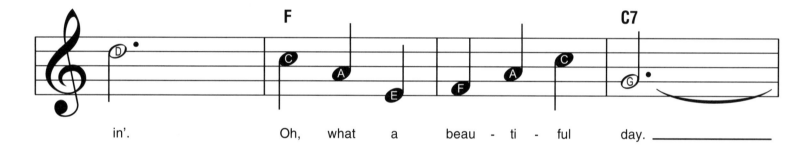

sky. Oh, what a beau - ti - ful morn -

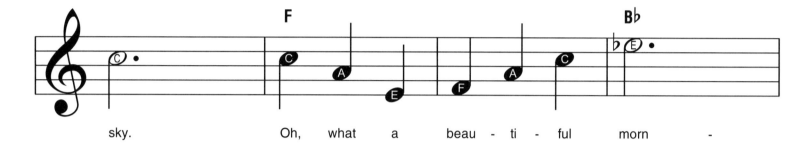

in'. Oh, what a beau - ti - ful day.

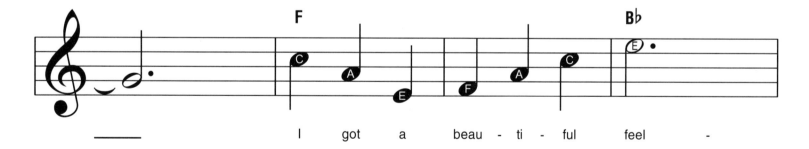

I got a beau - ti - ful feel -

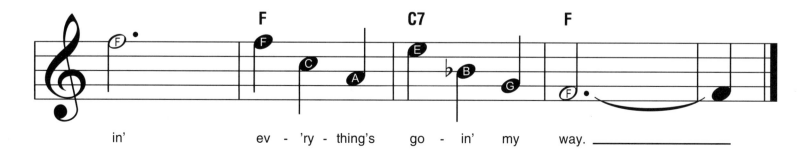

in' ev - 'ry - thing's go - in' my way.

100 Years

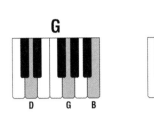
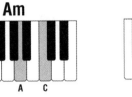

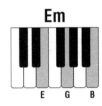
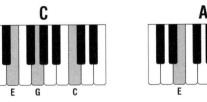

Words and Music by
John Ondrasik

Moderately fast

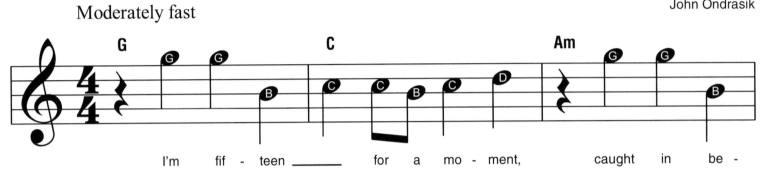

I'm fif - teen _____ for a mo - ment, caught in be -

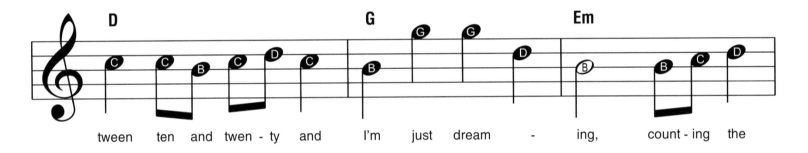

tween ten and twen - ty and I'm just dream - ing, count - ing the

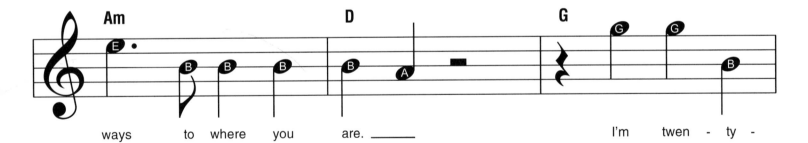

ways to where you are. _____ I'm twen - ty -

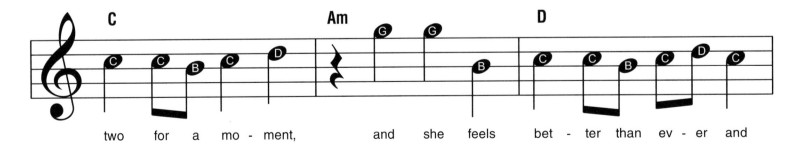

two for a mo - ment, and she feels bet - ter than ev - er and

we're on fire, _____ mak - ing our way back from

Mars. ____ Fif - teen, there's still time for

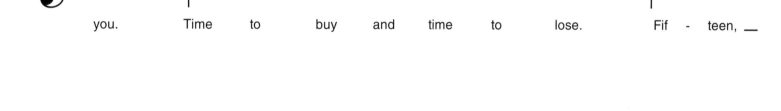

you. Time to buy and time to lose. Fif - teen, __

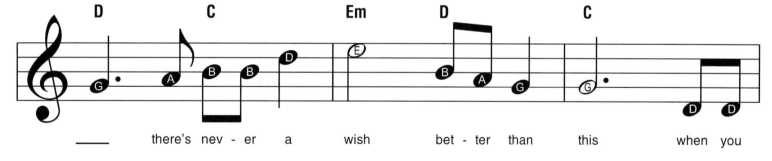

____ there's nev - er a wish bet - ter than this when you

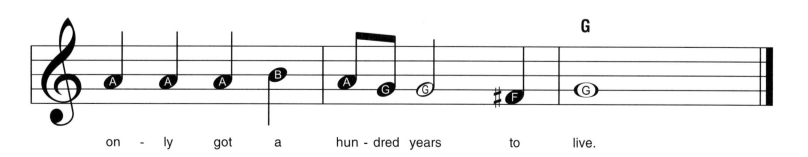

on - ly got a hun - dred years to live.

People Get Ready

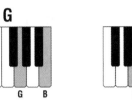 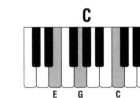

Words and Music by
Curtis Mayfield

Moderately

Peo - ple, get read - y; there's a train a - com - in'. You
Peo - ple, get read - y for the train to Jor - dan,

don't need no bag - gage; you just get on board. All you
pick - ing up pas - sen - gers from coast to coast.

need is faith to hear the die - sels hum - min'.
Faith is the key; o - pen the doors and board 'em.

Don't need no tick - et; you just thank the Lord.
There's hope for all a - mong those loved the most.

Release Me

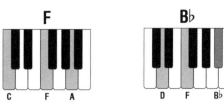 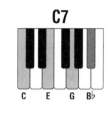

Words and Music by Robert Yount,
Eddie Miller and Dub Williams

Puff the Magic Dragon

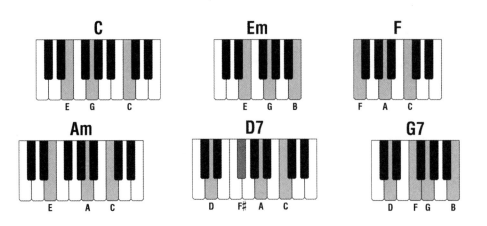

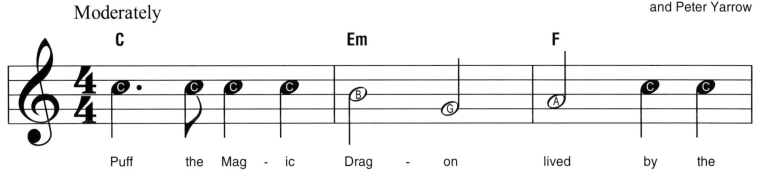

Words and Music by Lenny Lipton
and Peter Yarrow

Moderately

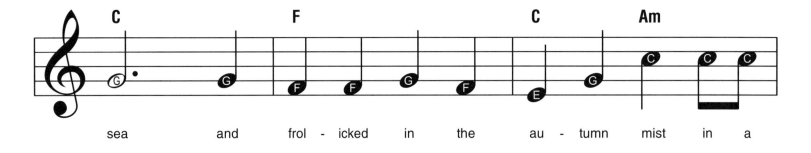

Puff the Mag - ic Drag - on lived by the

sea and frol - icked in the au - tumn mist in a

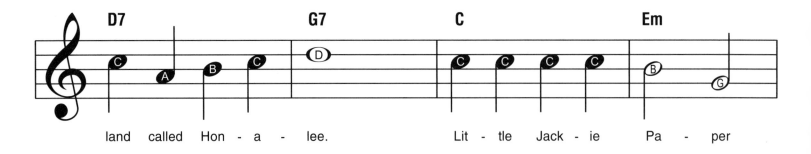

land called Hon - a - lee. Lit - tle Jack - ie Pa - per

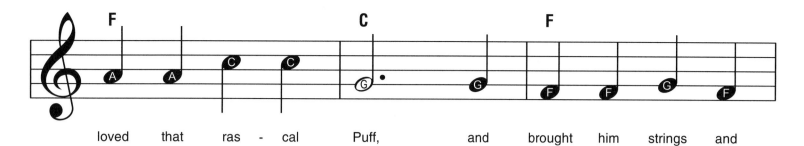

loved that ras - cal Puff, and brought him strings and

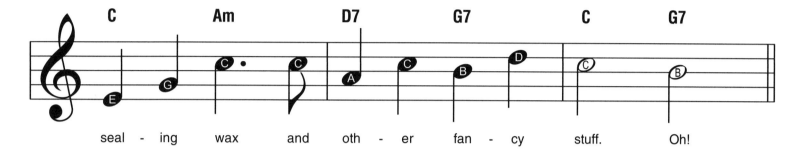

seal - ing wax and oth - er fan - cy stuff. Oh!

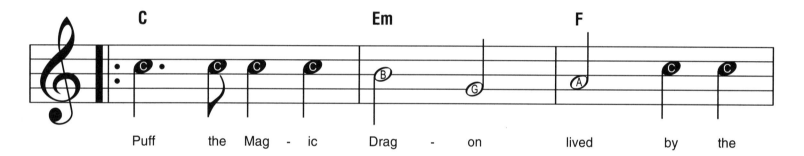

Puff the Mag - ic Drag - on lived by the

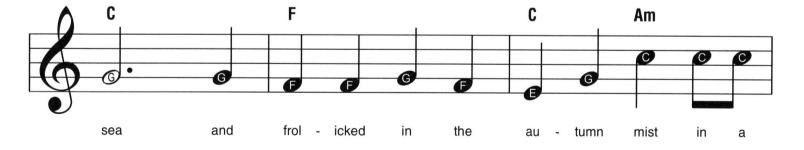

sea and frol - icked in the au - tumn mist in a

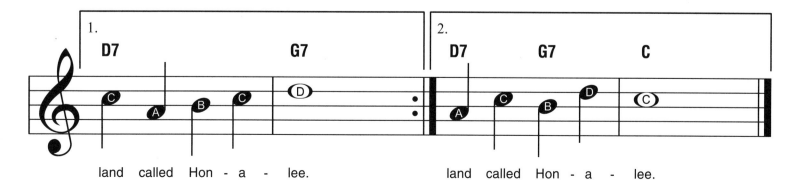

land called Hon - a - lee.   land called Hon - a - lee.

The Rainbow Connection
from THE MUPPET MOVIE

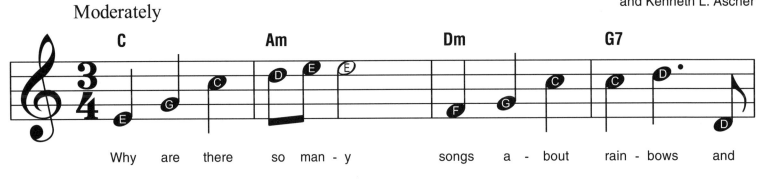

Words and Music by Paul Williams
and Kenneth L. Ascher

Moderately

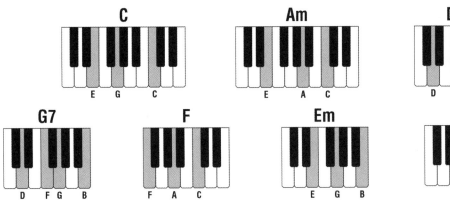
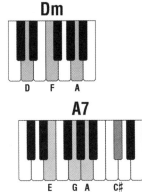

Why are there so man-y songs a-bout rain-bows and

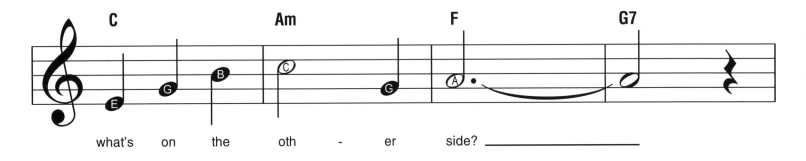

what's on the oth-er side? _____

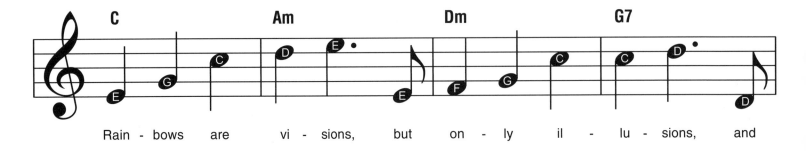

Rain-bows are vi-sions, but on-ly il-lu-sions, and

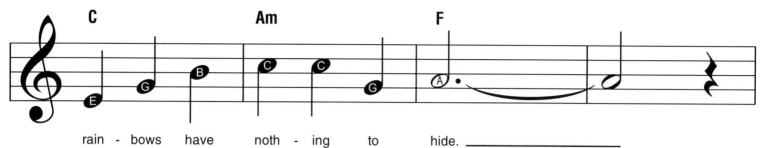

rain - bows have noth - ing to hide. _____

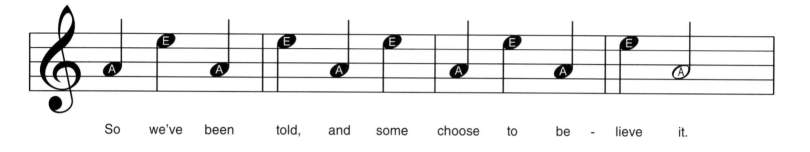

So we've been told, and some choose to be - lieve it.

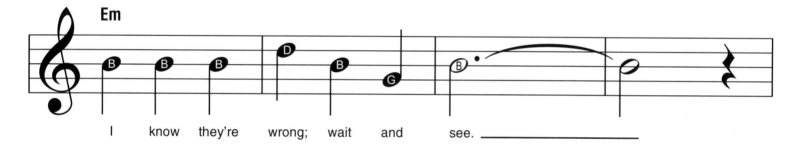

I know they're wrong; wait and see. _____

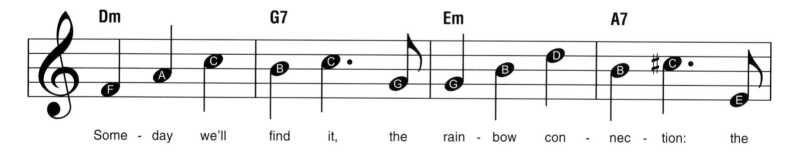

Some - day we'll find it, the rain - bow con - nec - tion: the

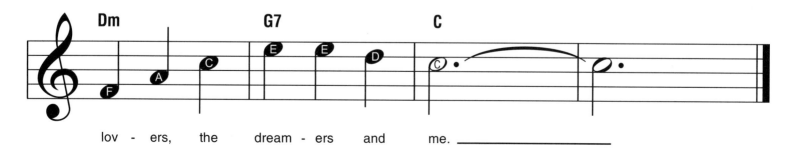

lov - ers, the dream - ers and me. _____

Right Here Waiting

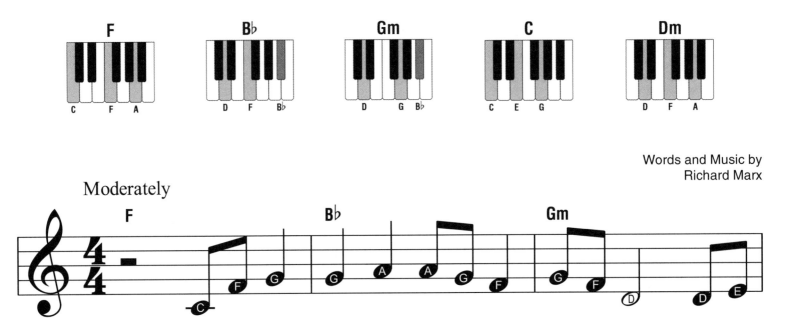

Words and Music by
Richard Marx

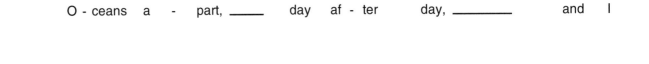

O - ceans a - part, ____ day af - ter day, _____ and I

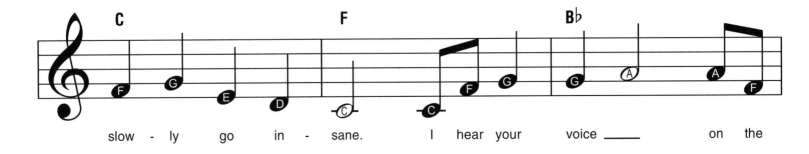

slow - ly go in - sane. I hear your voice ____ on the

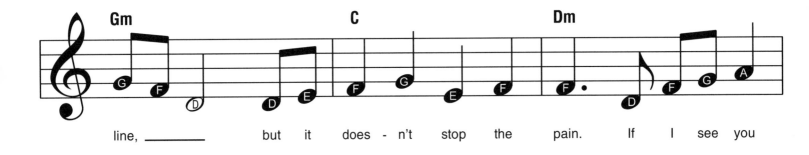

line, _____ but it does - n't stop the pain. If I see you

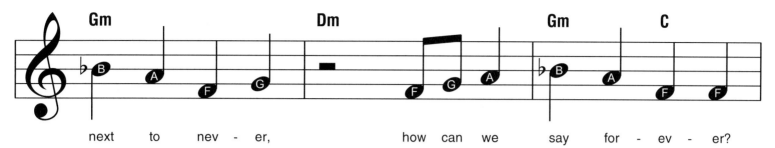

next to nev - er, how can we say for - ev - er?

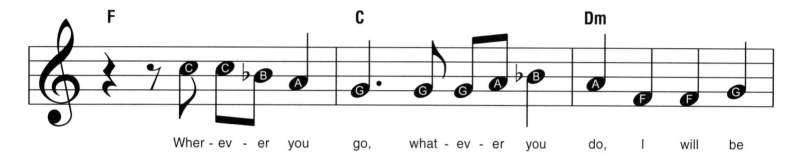

Wher - ev - er you go, what - ev - er you do, I will be

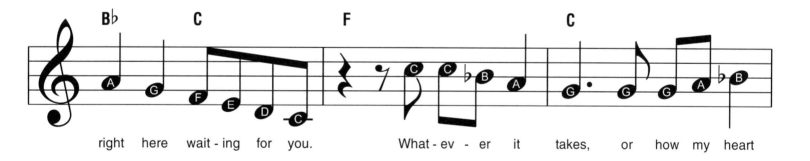

right here wait - ing for you. What - ev - er it takes, or how my heart

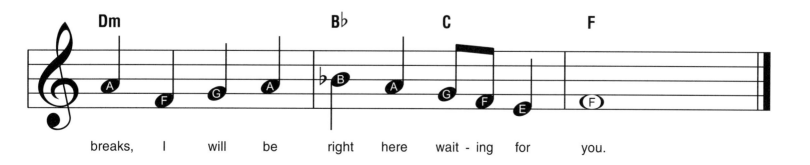

breaks, I will be right here wait - ing for you.

Rock Around the Clock

Words and Music by Max C. Freedman
and Jimmy DeKnight

Boogie-Woogie Shuffle

One, two, three o' - clock, four o' - clock rock.

Five, six, sev-en o - 'clock, eight o' - clock rock.

Nine, ten, e - lev-en o' - clock, twelve o' - clock rock. We're gon - na

rock a - round the clock to - night. Put your glad rags on and

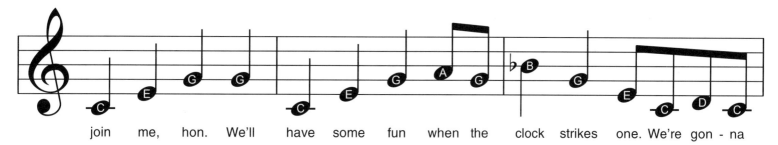

join me, hon. We'll have some fun when the clock strikes one. We're gon - na

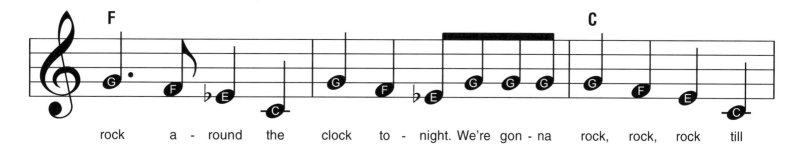

F   **C**

rock a - round the clock to - night. We're gon - na rock, rock, rock till

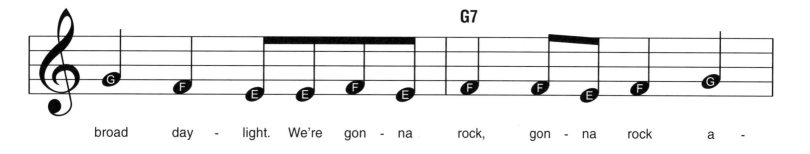

G7

broad day - light. We're gon - na rock, gon - na rock a -

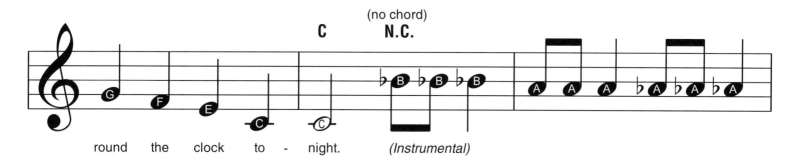

C   (no chord) **N.C.**

round the clock to - night. *(Instrumental)*

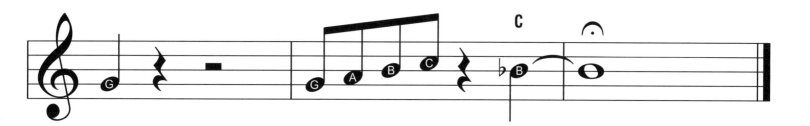

C

Rocky Top

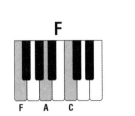
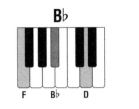

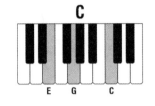
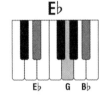

Words and Music by Boudleaux Bryant
and Felice Bryant

Brightly

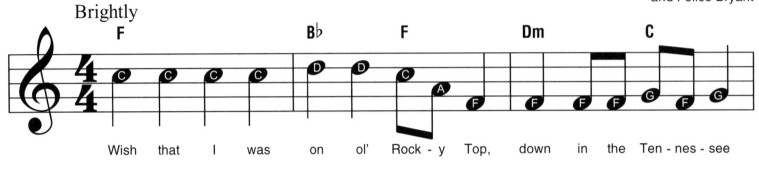

Wish that I was on ol' Rock-y Top, down in the Ten-nes-see

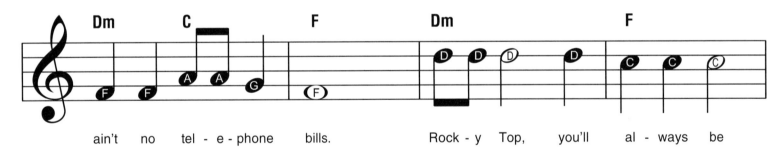

hills. Ain't no smog-gy smoke on Rock-y Top,

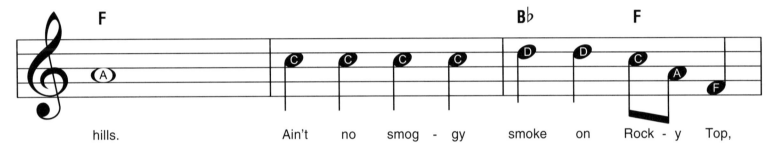

ain't no tel-e-phone bills. Rock-y Top, you'll al-ways be

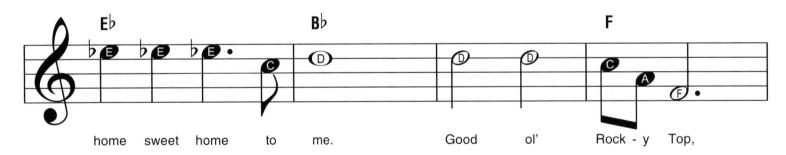

home sweet home to me. Good ol' Rock-y Top,

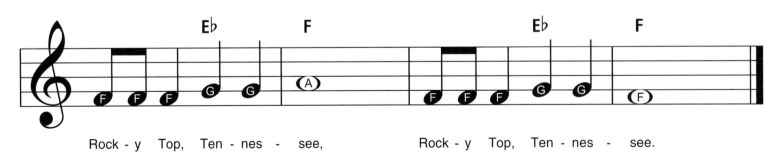

Rock-y Top, Ten-nes-see, Rock-y Top, Ten-nes-see.

When the Saints Go Marching In

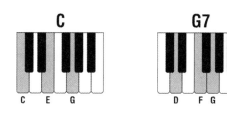
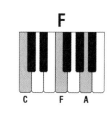

Words by Katherine E. Purvis
Music by James M. Black

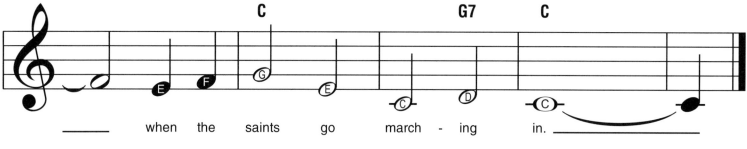

Route 66

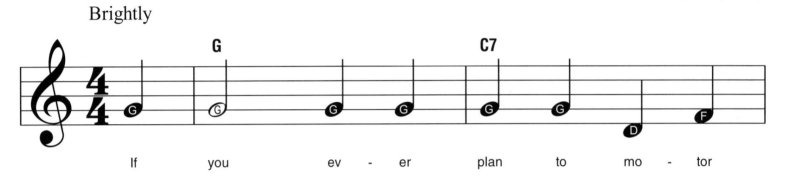

By Bobby Troup

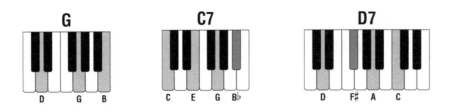

Brightly

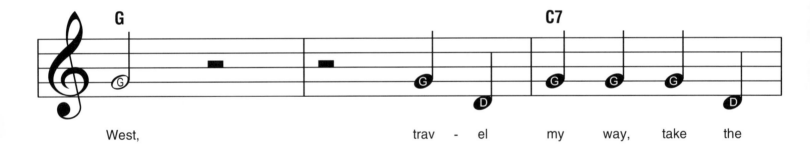

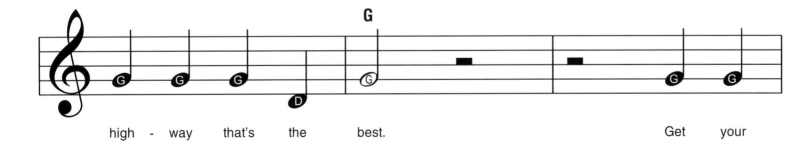

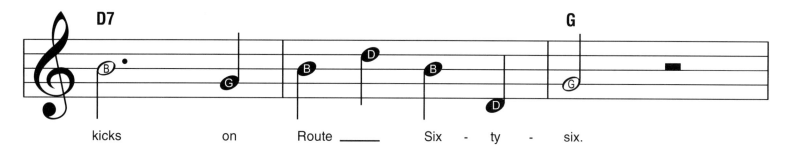

kicks   on   Route ____ Six - ty - six.

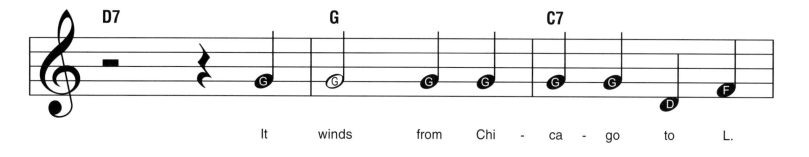

It   winds   from   Chi - ca - go   to   L.

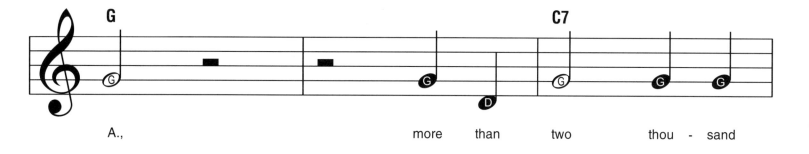

A.,   more   than   two   thou - sand

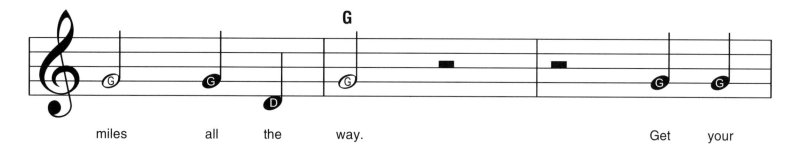

miles   all   the   way.   Get   your

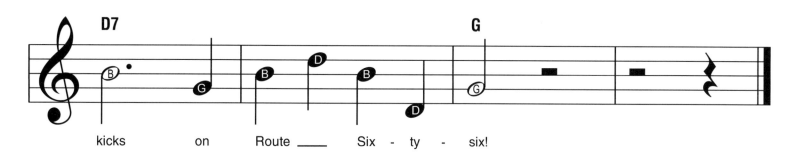

kicks   on   Route ____ Six - ty - six!

The Scientist

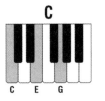
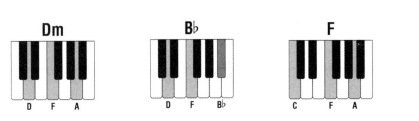

Words and Music by Guy Berryman,
Jon Buckland, Will Champion
and Chris Martin

Moderately slow

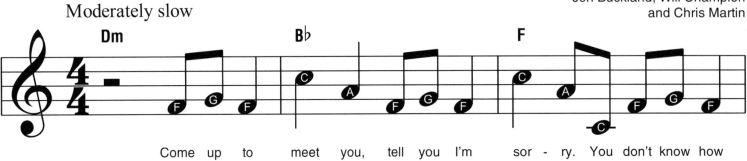

Come up to meet you, tell you I'm sor - ry. You don't know how

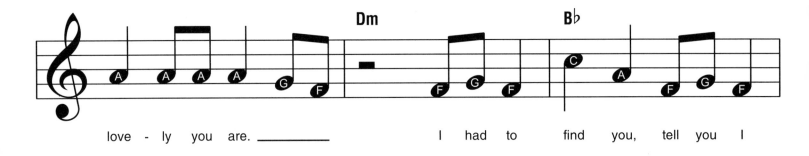

love - ly you are. _____ I had to find you, tell you I

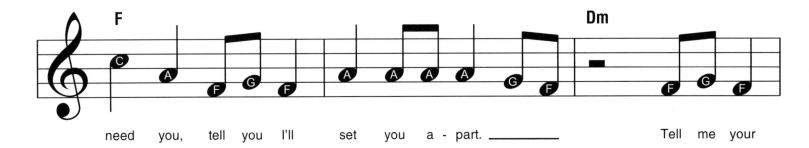

need you, tell you I'll set you a - part. _____ Tell me your

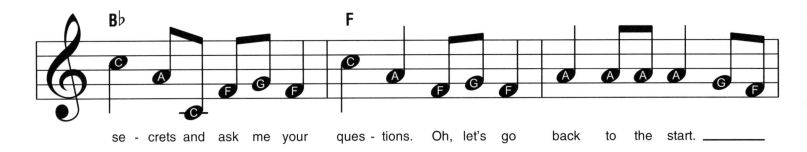

se - crets and ask me your ques - tions. Oh, let's go back to the start. _____

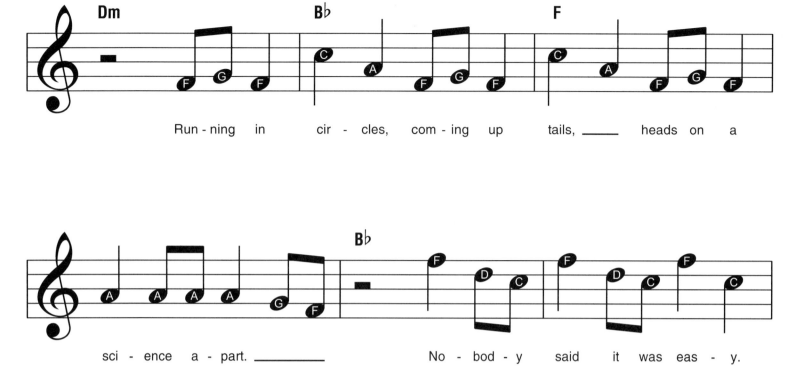

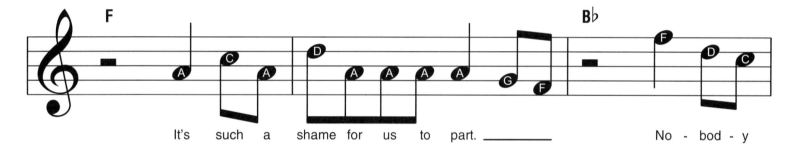

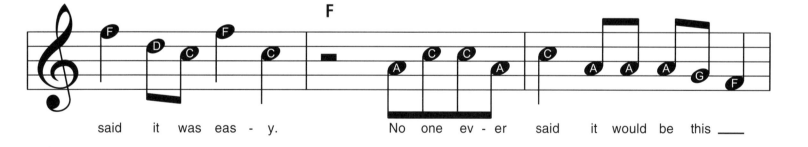

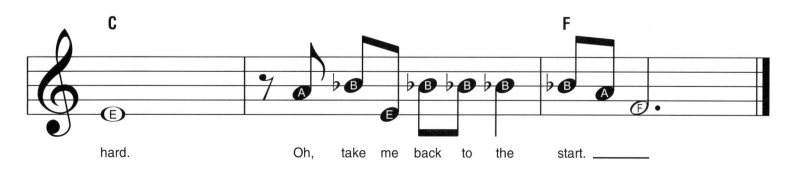

Simple Gifts

Traditional Shaker Hymn

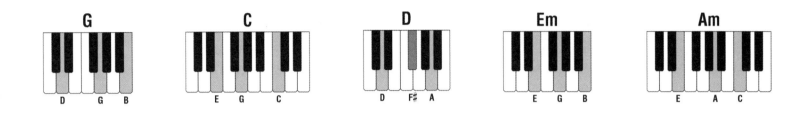

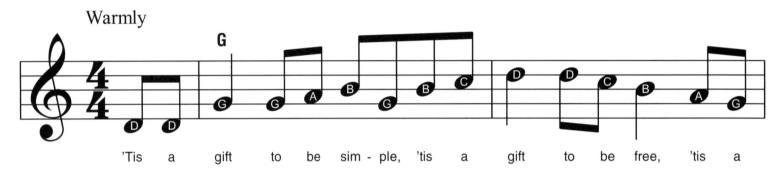

Warmly

'Tis a gift to be sim - ple, 'tis a gift to be free, 'tis a

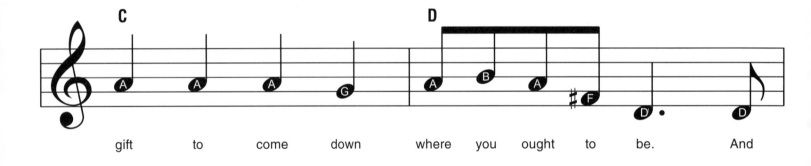

gift to come down where you ought to be. And

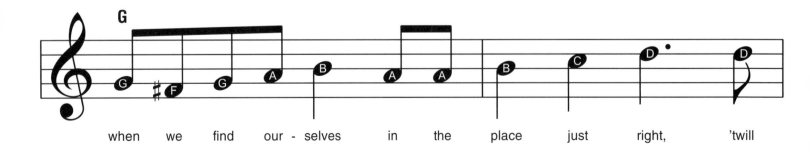

when we find our - selves in the place just right, 'twill

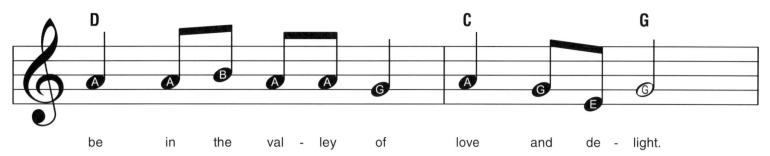

be in the val - ley of love and de - light.

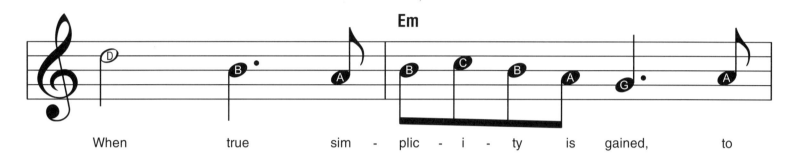

When true sim - plic - i - ty is gained, to

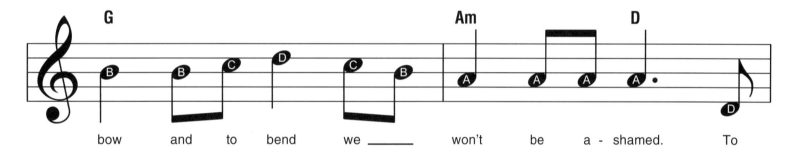

bow and to bend we _____ won't be a - shamed. To

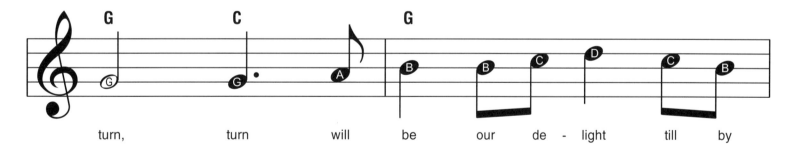

turn, turn will be our de - light till by

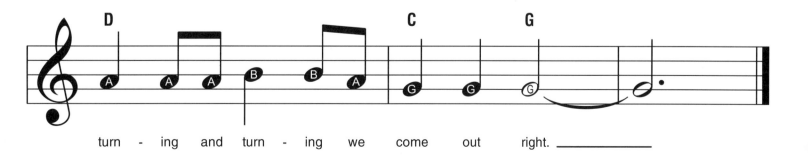

turn - ing and turn - ing we come out right. _____

Sing

from SESAME STREET

Words and Music by
Joe Raposo

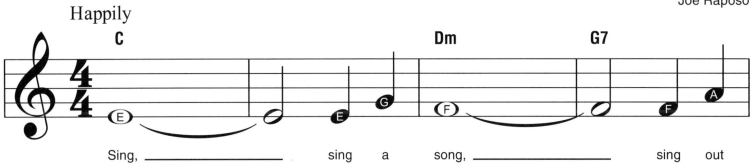

Sing, _____ sing a song, _____ sing out

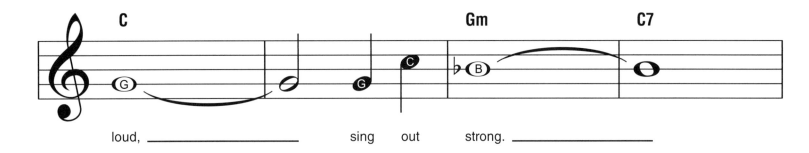

loud, _____ sing out strong. _____

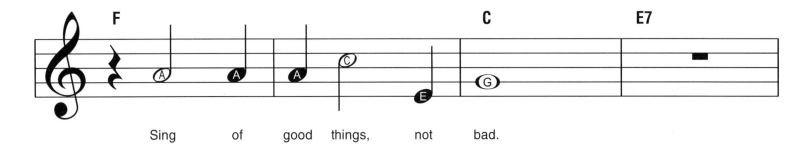

Sing of good things, not bad.

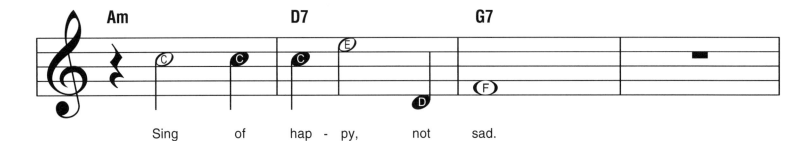

Sing of hap - py, not sad.

Somewhere, My Love
Lara's Theme from DOCTOR ZHIVAGO

Lyric by Paul Francis Webster
Music by Maurice Jarre

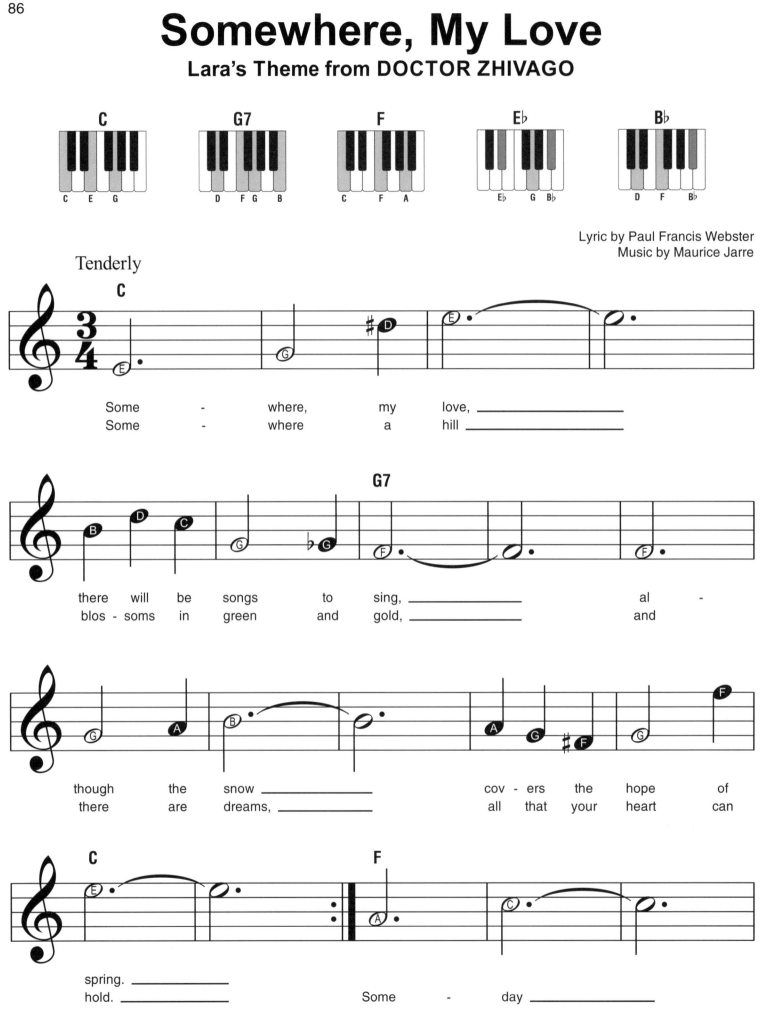

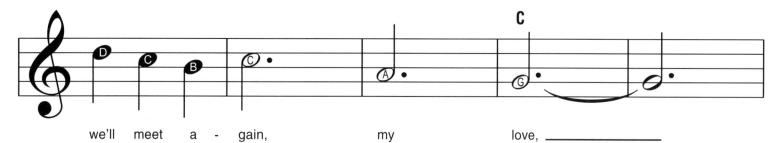

we'll meet a - gain, my love, _____

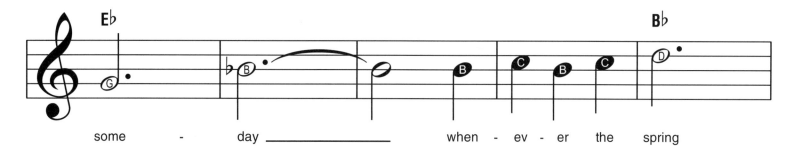

some - day _____ when - ev - er the spring

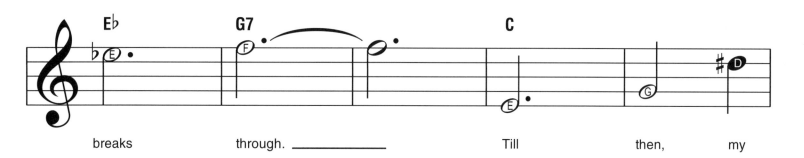

breaks through. _____ Till then, my

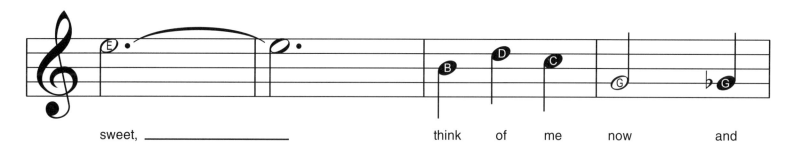

sweet, _____ think of me now and

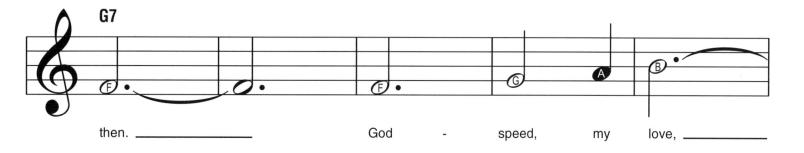

then. _____ God - speed, my love, _____

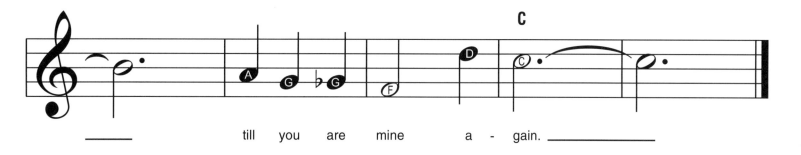

_____ till you are mine a - gain. _____

87

The Sound of Silence

from THE GRADUATE

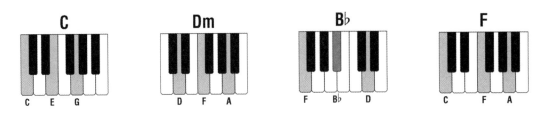

Words and Music by
Paul Simon

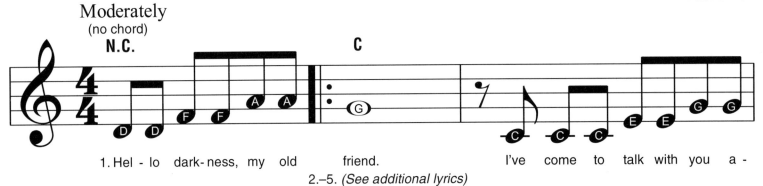

Moderately
(no chord)

1. Hel - lo dark - ness, my old friend.
2.–5. *(See additional lyrics)*

I've come to talk with you a-

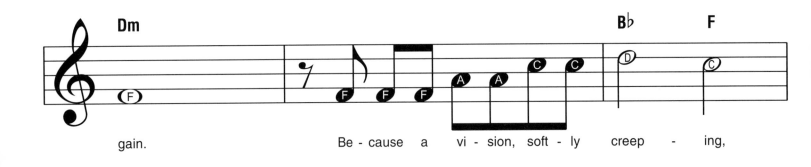

gain.

Be - cause a vi - sion, soft - ly creep - ing,

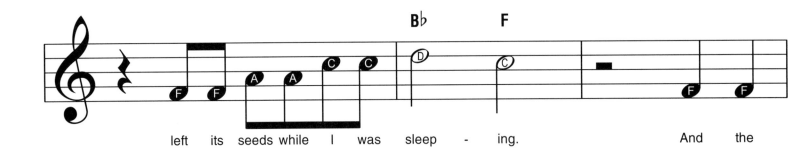

left its seeds while I was sleep - ing.

And the

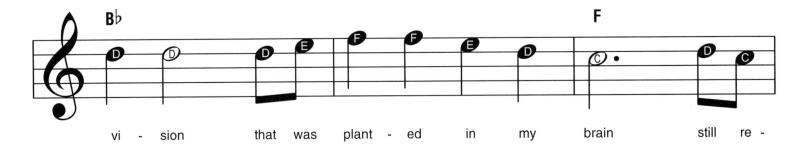

vi - sion that was plant - ed in my brain still re -

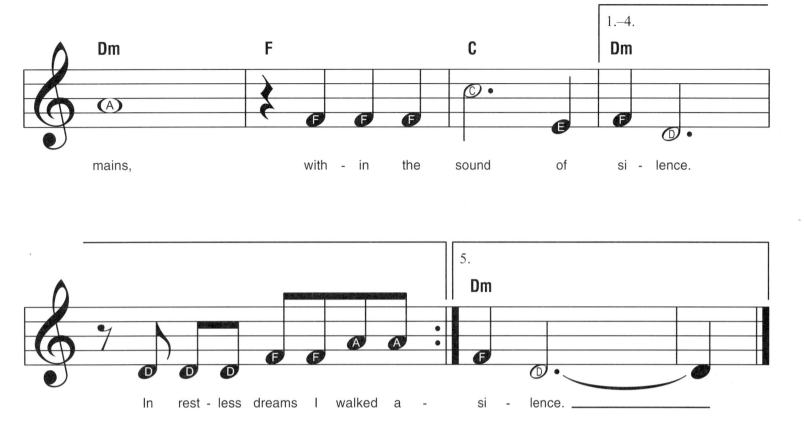

mains,   with - in the sound of si - lence.

In rest - less dreams I walked a - si - lence. _____

Additional Lyrics

2. In restless dreams I walked alone,
   Narrow streets of cobblestone.
   'Neath the halo of a street lamp,
   I turned my collar to the cold and damp.
   When my eyes were stabbed by the flash of a neon light
   That split the night, and touched the sound of silence.

3. And in the naked light I saw
   Ten thousand people, maybe more.
   People talking without speaking,
   People hearing without listening,
   People writing songs that voices never share.
   And no one dare disturb the sound of silence.

4. "Fools!" said I, "You do not know
   Silence, like a cancer, grows.
   Hear my words that I might teach you,
   Take my arms that I might reach you."
   But my words, like silent raindrops fell,
   And echoed in the wells of silence.

5. And the people bowed and prayed
   To the neon god they made.
   And the sign flashed out its warning,
   In the words that it was forming.
   And the sign said, "The words of the prophets
   Are written on the subway walls and tenement halls,
   And whispered in the sounds of silence."

Supercalifragilisticexpialidocious

from MARY POPPINS

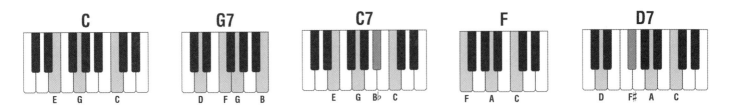

Words and Music by Richard M. Sherman
and Robert B. Sherman

Moderately fast

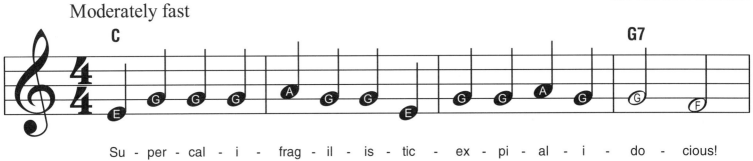

Su - per - cal - i - frag - il - is - tic - ex - pi - al - i - do - cious!

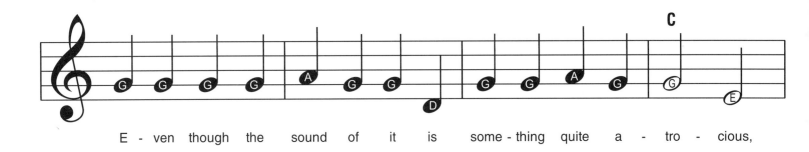

E - ven though the sound of it is some - thing quite a - tro - cious,

if you say it loud e - nough, you'll al - ways sound pre - co - cious.

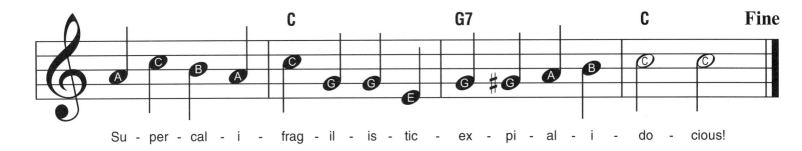

Su - per - cal - i - frag - il - is - tic - ex - pi - al - i - do - cious!

Sway
(Quien Será)

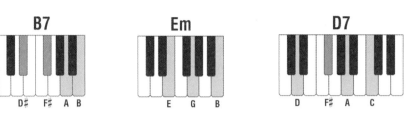

English Words by Norman Gimbel
Spanish Words and Music by Pablo Beltran Ruiz
and Luis Demetrio Traconis Molina

93

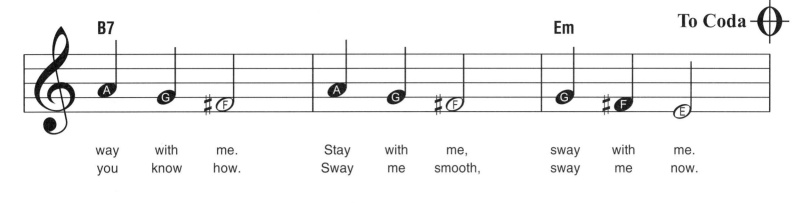

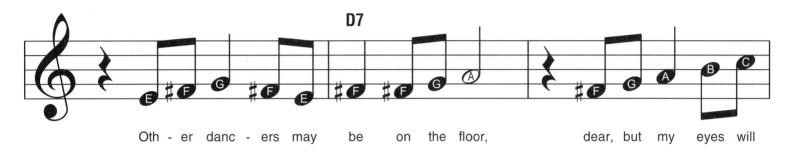

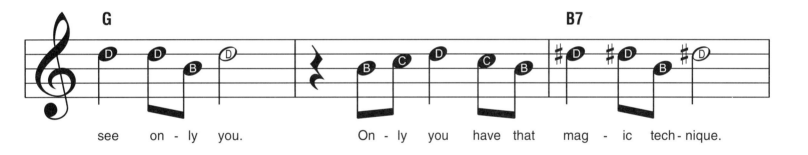

D.S. al Coda
(Return to 𝄋, play to ⊕
and skip to Coda)

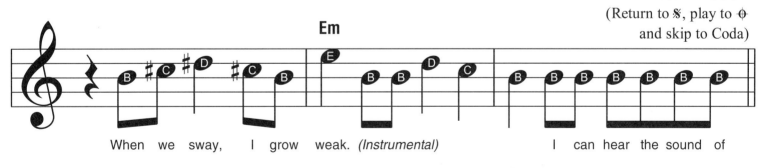

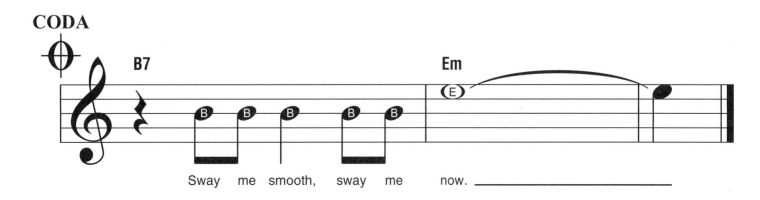

Sweet Caroline

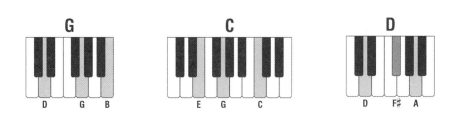

Words and Music by
Neil Diamond

Sweet Home Alabama

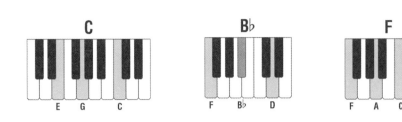

Words and Music by Ronnie Van Zant,
Ed King and Gary Rossington

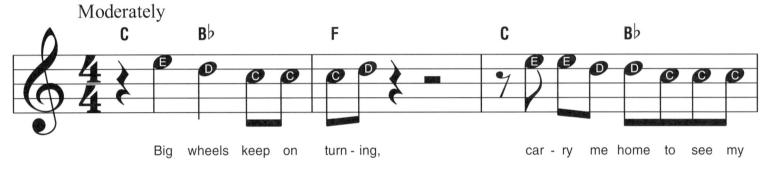

Big wheels keep on turn - ing,   car - ry me home to see my

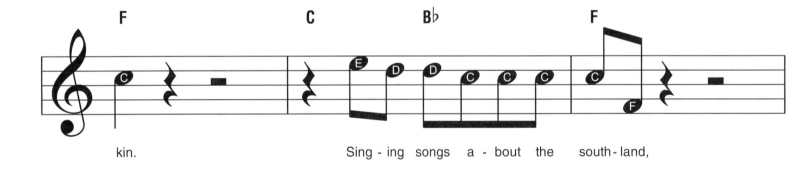

kin.   Sing - ing songs a - bout the south - land,

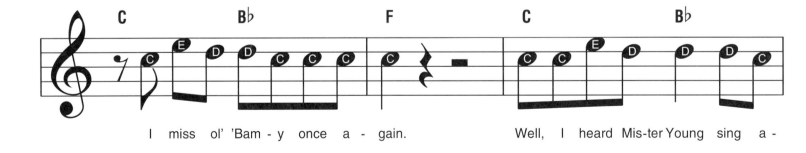

I miss ol' 'Bam - y once a - gain.   Well, I heard Mis-ter Young sing a-

Take Me Home, Country Roads

Words and Music by John Denver,
Bill Danoff and Taffy Nivert

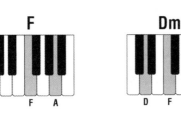
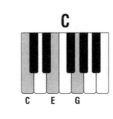
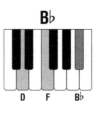

A Teenager in Love

Words by Doc Pomus
Music by Mort Shuman

Moderate half-time feel

1. Each time we have a quar-rel, it al - most
2., 3. *(See additional lyrics)*

breaks my heart, 'cause I am so a - fraid

that we will have to part. Each night I

ask the stars up a - bove: Why must I

be _____ a teen - ag - er in love?

Additional Lyrics

2. One day I feel so happy, next day I feel so sad.
I guess I'll learn to take the good with the bad.

3. If you want to make me cry, that won't be so hard to do.
And if you should say goodbye, I'll still go on loving you.

A Thousand Years
from the Summit Entertainment film
THE TWILIGHT SAGA: BREAKING DAWN - Part 1

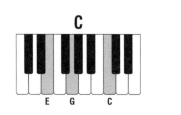
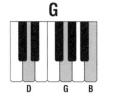
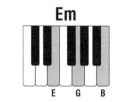

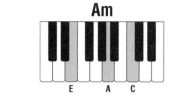

Words and Music by David Hodges
and Christina Perri

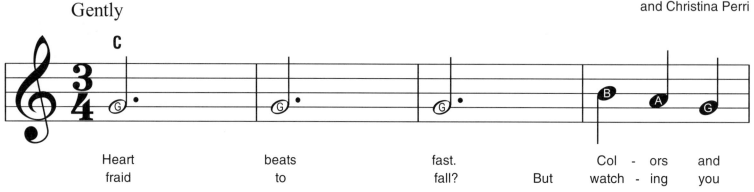

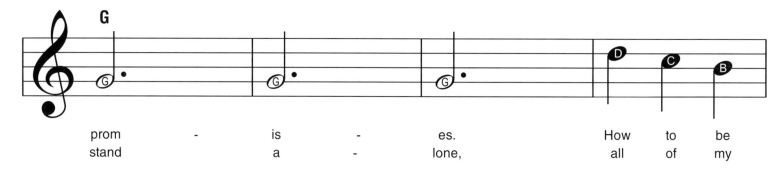

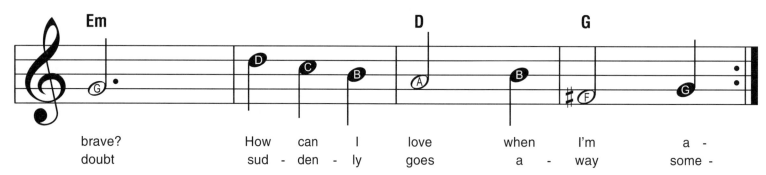

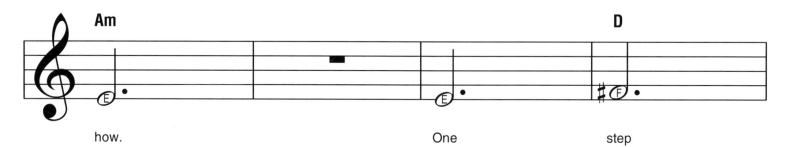

103

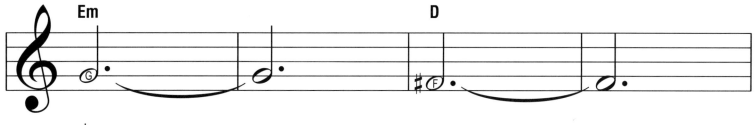

clos - er. _____

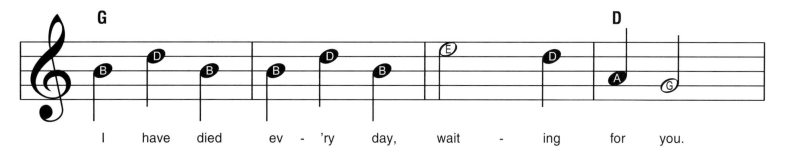

I have died ev - 'ry day, wait - ing for you.

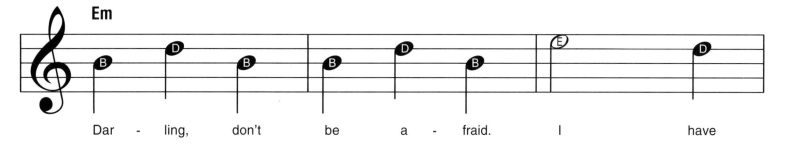

Dar - ling, don't be a - fraid. I have

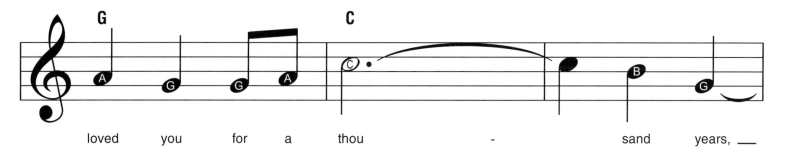

loved you for a thou - sand years, __

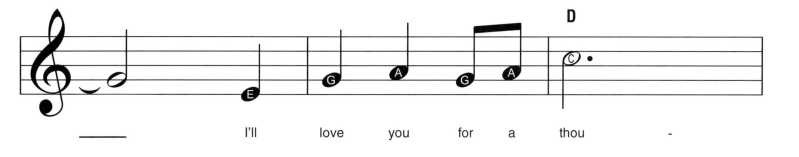

___ I'll love you for a thou -

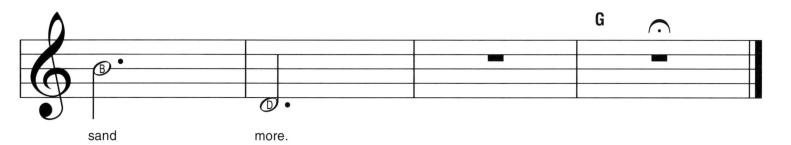

sand more.

Time for Me to Fly

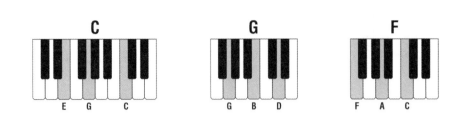

Words and Music by
Kevin Cronin

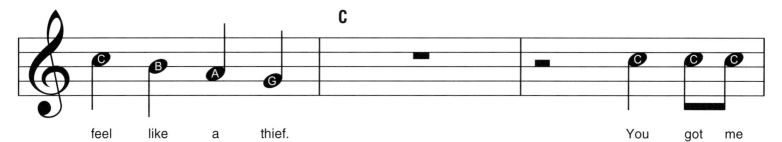

feel   like   a   thief.   You   got   me

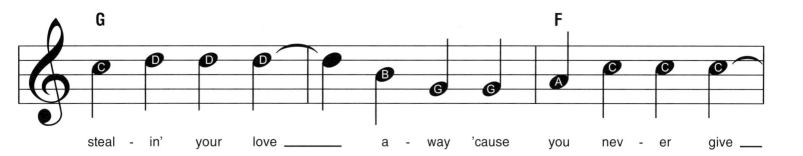

steal - in'   your   love _____   a - way   'cause   you   nev - er   give ___

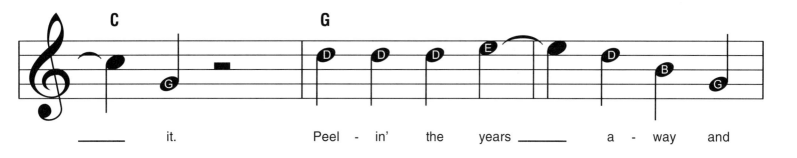

_____   it.   Peel - in'   the   years _____   a - way   and

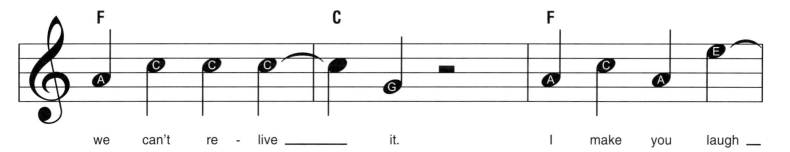

we   can't   re - live _____   it.   I   make   you   laugh __

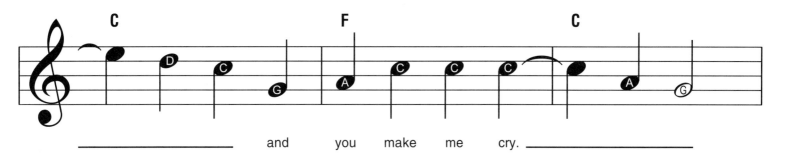

_____   and   you   make   me   cry. _____

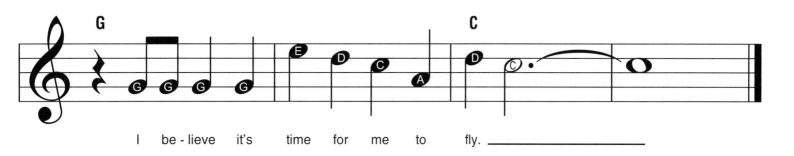

I   be - lieve   it's   time   for   me   to   fly. _____

Wonderful Tonight

Words and Music by
Eric Clapton

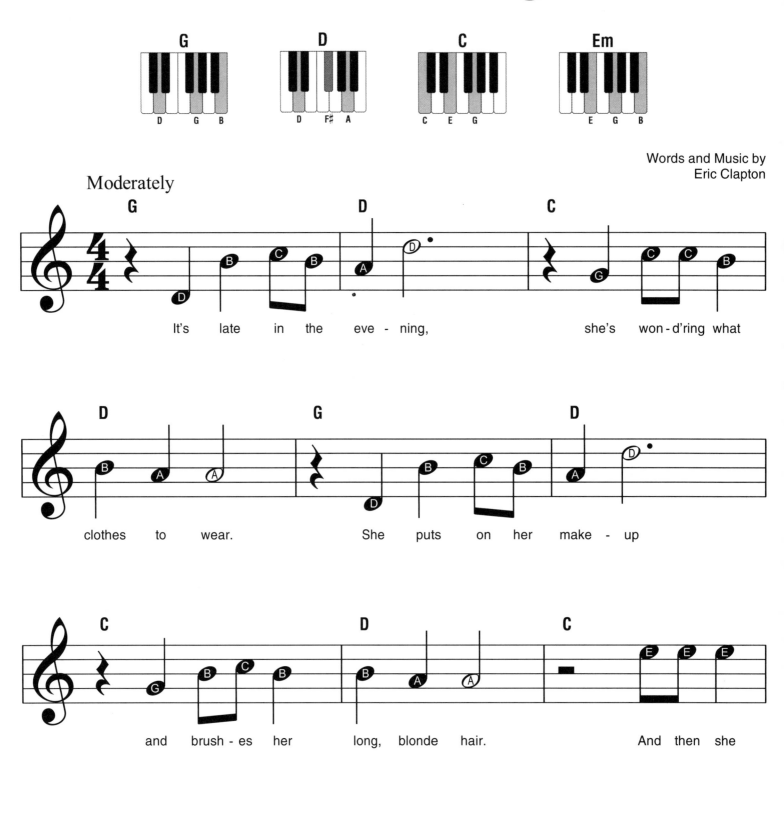

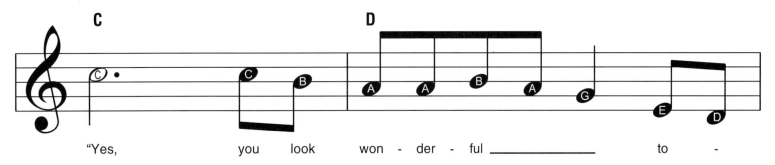

"Yes, you look won - der - ful ＿＿＿＿＿ to -

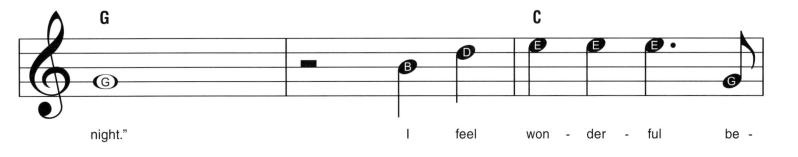

night." I feel won - der - ful be -

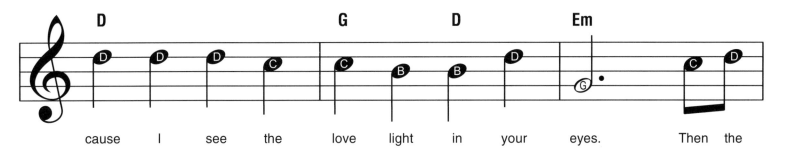

cause I see the love light in your eyes. Then the

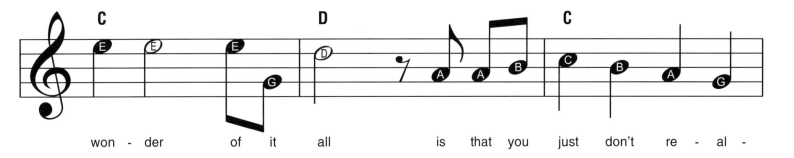

won - der of it all is that you just don't re - al -

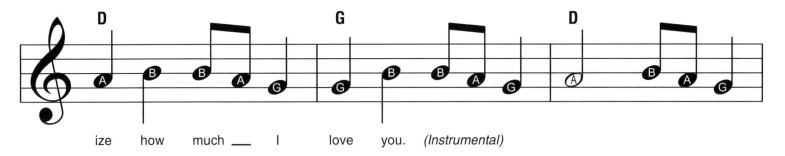

ize how much ＿ I love you. *(Instrumental)*

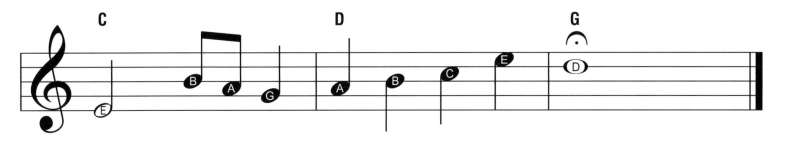

Yellow Submarine

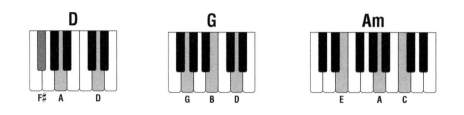

Words and Music by John Lennon
and Paul McCartney

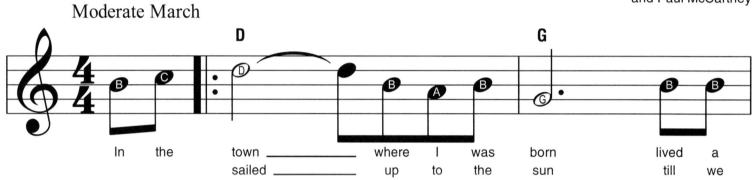

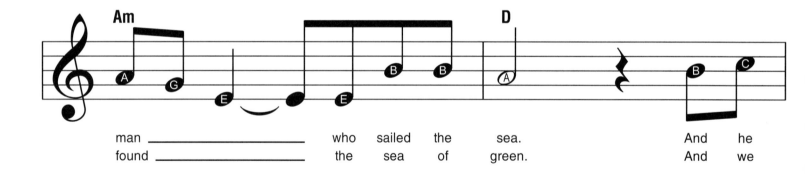

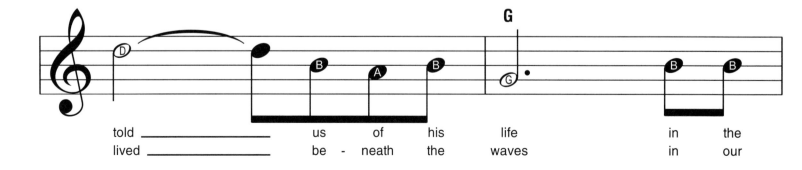

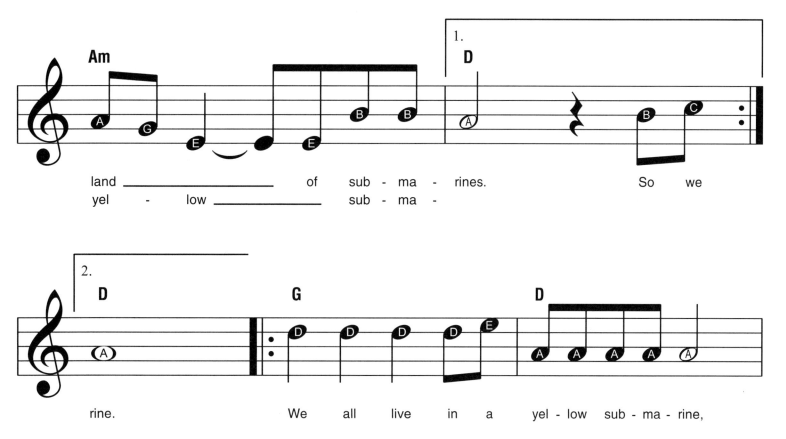

land _____ of sub - ma - rines.   So we
yel - low _____ sub - ma -

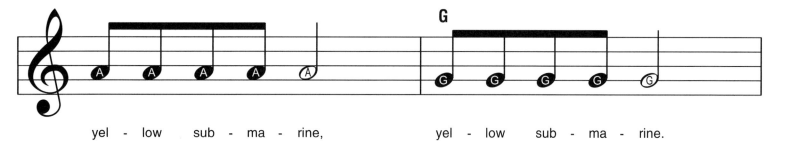

rine.   We all live in a yel - low sub - ma - rine,

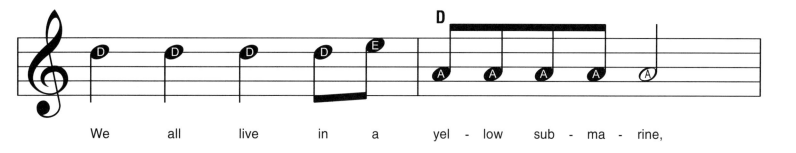

yel - low sub - ma - rine,   yel - low sub - ma - rine.

We all live in a yel - low sub - ma - rine,

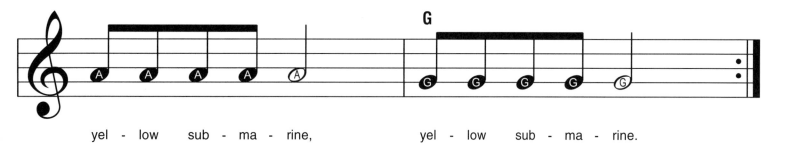

yel - low sub - ma - rine,   yel - low sub - ma - rine.

Your Cheatin' Heart

Words and Music by
Hank Williams

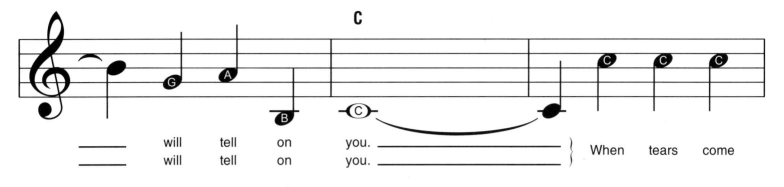

will tell on you. _____ When tears come

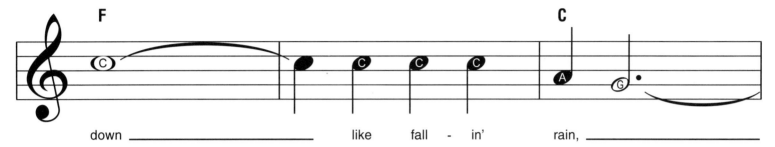

down _____ like fall - in' rain, _____

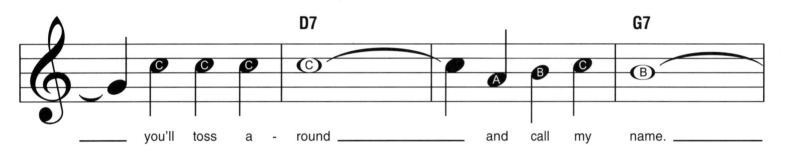

_____ you'll toss a - round _____ and call my name. _____

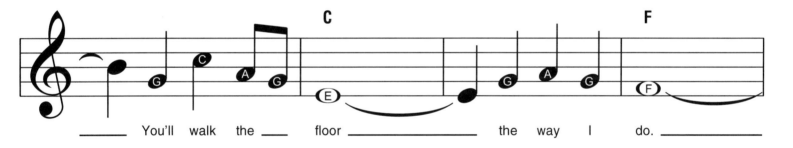

_____ You'll walk the ___ floor _____ the way I do. _____

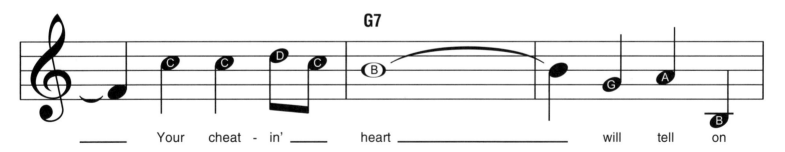

_____ Your cheat - in' ___ heart _____ will tell on

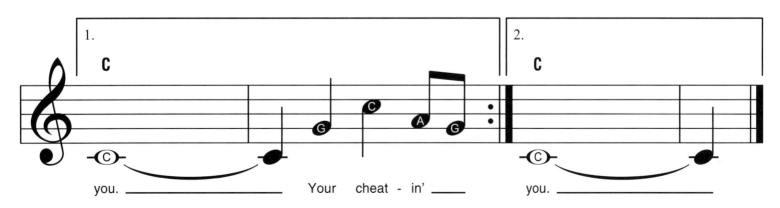

you. _____ Your cheat - in' ___ you. _____

You Are My Sunshine

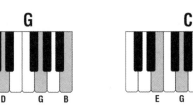  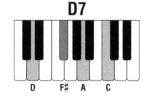

Words and Music by
Jimmie Davis